# Unconscious Marketing

*25 Cognitive Biases That Compel Your Customers To Buy (Without Them Knowing)*

## By Sam Page
### MBA, MPsych, MAPS

# TABLE OF CONTENTS

# FREE RESOURCES FROM SAM PAGE AND THE NEUROTRIGGERS TEAM

As an expression of gratitude for reading this book, I would like to offer you two FREE gifts so you can leverage the power of marketing psychology in your own business.

- **Visual Impact Map.** How well does your website engage your users' reptilian brain? Using predictive analysis, we'll present a full color map outlining your website's primary engagement points. *(Normally $129).*
- **Follow-up consultation and discovery session** (with a licensed consumer psychologist) to review your neuromarketing score. *(Normally $250).*

To claim these FREE gifts, just head on over to our website at www.NeuroTriggersAgency.com or shoot us an email at support@NeuroTriggersAgency.com.

# INTRODUCTION

How do you make important decisions in your life? If you're like most people, you'll probably give an answer such as:

- I make a list of pros and cons and consider it carefully, and then I decide based on which list is longer.
- I do research about all of my options, and then I use logic and deductive reasoning to make the best decision possible.
- I trust my gut instincts. I might do research or listen to arguments on both sides, but ultimately I go with my heart.

Chances are, whichever option you chose from that list, you truly believe that it describes how you make decisions. And unless you are a true anomaly, you're wrong.

## How Do People *Really* Make Decisions?

We all like to believe that logic, facts, and common sense play a role in our decision-making processes. But that's rarely the case. More often than not, we use mental shortcuts to help us evaluate the choices that are laid out before us. Sometimes these shortcuts are based on prior information, and sometimes they're based on faulty assumptions we make about the data we're working with.

These mental shortcuts are called cognitive biases, or heuristics. None of us are immune to them. We all use them in our decision-making process, whether we're aware we're doing it, or not. Some of these biases are so strong, that being aware of them does not lessen their effect. In one particular experiment, researchers informed participants of the mental bias they were about to be exposed to. Even with such foresight, participants were still helpless against it.

**What Does This Have to Do with Marketing?**

When you're designing a marketing campaign, your goal is always the same. After being exposed to your message, you want your target audience to take some of action (behavior). You might want them to sign up to your mailing list, or purchase your product, or pick up the phone and call you. You might want to steer them toward a particular service plan.

Whatever product or service you're marketing, everything you do is about getting customers to make a choice – and cognitive biases affect every choice we make.

When a carpenter sets out to build a house, he has tools to help him. He's got hammers and saws, nails and screws, and materials like wood, brick and tile. All of those tools are things he'll use to build a strong house that will provide shelter for the people who buy it. He couldn't do what he does without such tools.

Cognitive biases are tools for marketers. When you understand how cognitive biases work, you can use that information to construct marketing campaigns that will accomplish your goals more efficiently than any campaign you've ever designed before. You may find, as you read about these biases, some of them seem familiar. You may have fallen victim to their forces before. You may have even employed them in your own marketing campaigns, consciously or otherwise. The more you understand about cognitive biases and how they affect consumer decision-making, the better equipped you'll be to use them strategically.

## How Do Cognitive Biases Work?

Everyone is different. For example, some people may be more susceptive to a cognitive bias called the Bandwagon Effect, which compels one to follow along with whatever the majority is doing. Others may find themselves disposed to the base-rate fallacy, which we'll discuss a little later. The more intimately you know your audience, the more purposefully, and effectively, you can employ certain biases and heuristics.

You can use cognitive biases to:

- Overcome perceptions of anticipatory purchase regret
- Prevent choice-set complexity and decision paralysis
- Increase your brand loyalty and brand equity
- Convert customers into ambassadors for your brand
- And much, much more…

Interestingly, there are some cognitive biases that marketers have to watch out for as much as customers do. When that happens, we'll make note of it so you can be on the lookout for your own reactions and learn how to avoid making mental shortcuts that undercut the effectiveness of your own campaigns.

## What You'll Learn

This book has detailed information about twenty-five of the most common cognitive biases, the ones that are most useful to marketers. You'll get a simple explanation of what the bias is and how it works, and some background on the research that supports it. After that, we'll explain how to use the bias within your marketing campaigns, and give you some real world examples and ideas. Because B2B marketing and B2C marketing each have their own unique challenges, we'll discuss the application for each, separately. By the end of the book, you'll have a firm grasp on how to start using cognitive biases in your marketing to increase sales, conversions, and customer loyalty.

For people who don't understand how they work, cognitive biases can seem almost like magic. How can a marketer know that a consumer is more likely to pick one subscription offer over another? How can we overcome a client's reluctance to try something new? How can we know which pieces of information a potential client is likely to notice, and which things they'll likely skip over? Understanding cognitive biases is about understanding the human brain and how it works. Once you're privy to this, you can tailor any marketing campaign to your target customers in a way that's seamless and effective.

You might be thinking; *"isn't this manipulation?"*

The answer is yes, it is. You're strategically modifying one's perception, and ultimately their behavior, to generate more sales for your business.

Now, this book is not for beginners in business. It's not for the unscrupulous, nor the stupid. It's for the intelligent marketer who has a great product/service, and who provides exponentially more value *to* the market, than that which they derive *from* the market. That is all to say; the cognitive biases outlined herein, provide the foundation for ethical manipulation. A force for good.

# ANGELS IN ADVERTISING: UNDERSTANDING THE HALO EFFECT

Have you ever been in a supermarket or pharmacy and found yourself wavering between two brands? They might be similar in many ways, but chances are that if one of the two brands has been endorsed by a celebrity you admire, you'll choose that brand in the end. You might not even be aware that you made the decision you did because of the celebrity endorsement, and that hardly makes you unusual. It's an example of a cognitive bias known as the *Halo Effect*.

## What Is the Halo Effect?

The Halo Effect is one of many cognitive biases that affect the way we process information and make decisions. It was first described by a psychologist named Edward Thorndike back in 1920 in his paper, A Constant Error in Psychological Ratings.[1] In it, he asked military commanders to rate men under their command based on a variety of characteristics, including physical qualities, leadership skills, intellect, and personal qualities.

What he found is that there was an unusually high correlation in the ratings across all categories. If the commanders had a high opinion of a man's physical abilities, their ratings were correspondingly higher across all categories, and the same was true if they had a strong negative opinion. He called it the Halo Effect because the one quality with the highest rating cast a halo over the rest of the person's qualities, whether it was warranted or not.

## The Halo Effect and Marketing

You might wonder what rating the personal qualities of men in the military has to do with marketing. The Halo Effect works in all areas of life. We are far more likely to assume the best about attractive people – in other words, their physical attractiveness casts a halo over their other qualities. We are more inclined to assume that a handsome man is intelligent and that an unattractive man is unintelligent.

Let's look at a case study about the popular brand, Wonder Bread.[2] They were the subject of a lawsuit that claimed they had misrepresented the nutritional quality of their product. The case was eventually dismissed, but research showed that customers had vastly overestimated the nutritional content of the bread because they had an overall positive impression of the brand based on things like familiarity and price. Thus, in this case, the Halo Effect carried over from a perception of the brand being affordable to one of it also being nutritional – whether or not that was true.

Another common way marketers make use of the Halo Effect is by licensing the rights to a popular song and using it in a commercial.[3] Viewers who see the commercial will likely correlate their enjoyment of the song with the product itself. The Halo Effect is also the reason why politicians use popular songs – sometimes without permission – in their campaign appearances.

**Examples of the Halo Effect in Action**

The Halo Effect is used by marketers all the time. Let's look at some examples in B2C marketing:

1. Perhaps the single most famous example of the Halo Effect is the old Vicks 44 commercial that featured the line, "I'm not a doctor, but I play one on TV." That

ad used the popularity of actor Chris Robinson, who played a doctor on General Hospital, to sell cough syrup. Advertisers have used variations on the "I'm a doctor" line ever since.

2. A recent example features actress Jennifer Aniston talking about her skin care secrets in an ad for Aveeno products. The ad plays off of Aniston's beauty and likability to sell the product. Consumers are more likely to buy it because of their generally positive feelings about the actress.[4]

3. When a company introduces a new product, its popularity can lift the company as a whole. A classic example is the way Apple's sales rose 384% in 2005 after they released the iPod. A company may choose to advertise only its most popular product (or its most affordable one) knowing that one runaway success can lift the whole brand.

The Halo Effect is also used in B2B marketing:

1. Deloitte, an international consulting and accounting firm, sponsors what they call "Impact Day", once a year. On that day, more than 10,000 employees volunteer their time to charities. While they don't

specifically advertise the fact that they do it, they do provide employees with t-shirts to wear while they are volunteering. Everyone who sees the t-shirts associates Deloitte with giving back to the community – a halo that then extends to their business services as well.

2. Celebrity endorsements aren't just for B2C marketing. When handled properly, they can work for B2B as well. One recent example is the Hewlett-Packard campaign featuring musician and fashion designer Gwen Stefani. The tagline for the commercial was, "The computer is personal again." The target audience for the commercial was small to medium-sized companies and the graphic arts community. Stefani's popularity and young, hip image, helped HP reinvent itself.

In general, the Halo Effect works best when the connection between the celebrity endorser or charitable effort and the company is strong. An example of this is Wells Fargo's "The Fun in Money" campaign, which travels to college campuses giving advice about personal finances to new graduates. The bank is giving back in an area that is directly connected to their primary business – banking – and as a result they reap the full benefit of the Halo Effect.

The key to using the Halo Effect well is to choose wisely. It won't do you any good to associate your product with a hot young star if he's regularly getting arrested for drunk and disorderly behavior. If you base your relationship on a connection that customers can make easily, then you can be confident that the Halo Effect will work for you.

## CITATIONS

1. Thorndike, E. L. (1920). A constant error in psychological ratings. *Journal of applied psychology*, *4*(1), 25-29.
2. Beckwith, N. E., Kassarjian, H. H., & Lehmann, D. R. (1978). Halo effects in marketing research: Review and prognosis. *Advances in consumer research*, *5*(1), 465-467.
3. Bruner, G. C. (1990). Music, mood, and marketing. *the Journal of marketing*, 94-104.
4. Dean, D. H. (1999). Brand endorsement, popularity, and event sponsorship as advertising cues affecting consumer pre-purchase attitudes. *Journal of Advertising*, *28*(3), 1-12.

# ATTENTIONAL BIAS:
# WHY WE NOTICE WHAT WE NOTICE

Imagine that you're talking to a friend. In the middle of your conversation, she uses a word you've never heard before. You ask her what it means, and she tells you. Later on that same day, you're reading an article online, and you come across that same word. It seems strange to you because you just learned it for the first time, and now you've encountered it twice in the same day. What are the chances? You're even more amazed when you read it a third time later that week.

What's going on? Did everyone else just learn the word too? Why is it everywhere? The answer is simple. The word isn't being used any more frequently than it was before you learned what it meant, but now it's drawing your attention in a new way. This phenomenon is a cognitive bias known as *Attentional Bias*.

## Understanding Attentional Bias

Intuitively, you know that it's not possible to pay attention to everything. The average person encounters countless numbers of stimuli on a given day, and most of them pass by unnoticed. If they didn't, we'd all be walking around with sensory overload. Attentional Bias was first studied by researchers Colin MacLeod, Andrew Mathews and Philip Tata in 1986. Their study focused on people with anxiety disorder.[1] They showed a mix of anxiety-inducing images and neutral images to people with anxiety disorder and a control group. They found that the people who were predisposed to anxiety paid more attention to the anxiety-inducing pictures than the control group did.

A 1993 study explored the same phenomenon among a different group: people with arachnophobia (fear of spiders.)[2] Once again, the study showed that people with a fear of spiders paid significantly more attention to images of spiders than people who did not.

Attentional Bias does not apply only to images – it applies to words, too. A 1998 study separated participants into two groups: people who were hungry, and people who were not. Each group was then presented with a series of words to read, some of which were food-related. The hungry group paid far more attention to the food-related words than the group that was not hungry.[3]

The lesson here is that the things that are already in our heads are the things we notice the most. When you learn a new word, or you have a fear, the word or the subject of your fear is already taking up space in your brain. That means you're more likely to notice them.

## Attentional Bias in Marketing

The key takeaway for marketers from Attentional Bias is that once you are in a customer's head, they are more likely to notice you. This can work for you in several ways. It can help to increase brand awareness and loyalty, and when you turn it the other way, paying attention to your clients can improve customer service.

Some ways to use Attentional Bias in marketing include maintaining an active social media presence, having a blog on your company website and updated it frequently, and retargeting customers who have visited your website but not yet made a purchase.

## Examples of Attentional Bias in Marketing

Attentional Bias can be used in a number of different ways to help your business, whether you are marketing B2B or B2C. Sometimes marketing techniques can vary greatly depending on your audience, but this is one cognitive bias that can work in the same ways regardless of who your customers are. All of the following techniques can work for B2B or B2C marketing. Let's look at some examples:

1. Retargeting is a form of advertising that allows marketers to display ads to customers who have visited their website but not yet made a purchase. Amazon does this all the time, but it could be very effective for almost any product or service. You can specify that you want your ad to target people who have abandoned items in the shopping cart of your online store. Google AdWords allows you to do this kind of marketing, and it can be very effective at getting people to come back and complete a purchase.

The Attentional Bias comes into play because your company is already on their mind.

2. Social media marketing is another effective way to use Attentional Bias to capture customers. When a customer chooses to like your Facebook page or follow you on Twitter, you know that they're aware of your product or brand. You can then use your social media presence to continually draw attention to yourself, thus increasing the chances that they'll make a purchase. This technique can work using paid advertising as well as free social media techniques like Tweets and status updates.

3. Many internet marketers use repeated Calls to Action (CTAs) on their web pages. Each CTA draws attention to the action you want people to take, and the attention they pay to each one increases as your CTA takes up more space in their brains. This is particularly effective on long-form pages where you have a lot of content, and it can work for both B2B and B2C marketing. Incidentally, repeated CTAs can be effective in email marketing, too.

4. Blogging can be a very effective way of triggering Attentional Bias in your customers. Many companies have a regular blog on their web site, but some don't.

When you blog – and especially if you offer a way for readers to subscribe to your blog, or if you share your blog on social media – you are making sure that your company has some mental real estate in your customers' brains. Attentional Bias means they'll be more likely to engage with your content, and to share it with their friends.

5. Finally, you can use Attentional Bias to increase your employees' engagement with clients. One company has employees read clients' blogs on a regular basis. Reading the blog keeps the client at the forefront of their minds, and it has a marked effect on the quality of customer service. That's not marketing in the traditional sense, but it can certainly help with customer satisfaction and retention.

Attentional Bias is something that affects us all. The key to using it is to understand that your customers have a limited amount of attention to spare at any given time. When you make a point of keeping your brand in front of them, it's more likely that they'll give you their attention.

# CITATIONS

1. MacLeod, C., Mathews, A., & Tata, P. (1986). Attentional bias in emotional disorders. *Journal of abnormal psychology*, *95*(1), 15.

2. Lavy, E., Van den Hout, M., & Arntz, A. (1993). Attentional bias and spider phobia: Conceptual and clinical issues. *Behaviour Research and Therapy*, *31*(1), 17-24.

3. Mogg, K., Bradley, B. P., Hyare, H., & Lee, S. (1998). Selective attention to food-related stimuli in hunger: are attentional biases specific to emotional and psychopathological states, or are they also found in normal drive states?. *Behaviour research and therapy*, *36*(2), 227-237.

# BASE-RATE FALLACY:
# HARD-WIRED FOR JUDGMENT

If you're like most people, you think that, in situations where you have access to statistical data and facts, the factual information will play a role in your decision-making process. The truth is that we're far more likely to be swayed by our preconceived ideas than we are by numbers.

For example, imagine that you are attending a street fair with ten thousand other people. As you walk down the street, someone hands you a pamphlet advising you to watch out for pickpockets – solid advice in any crowd situation. The pamphlet isn't just a warning, though; it's got data to back it up. It informs you that of the people in attendance, ten are pickpockets. That means that the probability of any one person being a pickpocket is .0001, or one in a thousand.

A few minutes later, someone comes up to you and points out a particular person in the crowd. This person is wearing threadbare clothes, and her hair is a bit messy. They ask you to assess the probability that this one person is a pickpocket.

Chances are, you're going to come up with a number that's higher than .0001. There's no logical basis for you to draw such a conclusion – it's based entirely on your preconceived notion of what a pickpocket looks like. In other words, you ignored the statistics and arrived at a completely illogical conclusion. That's the Base Rate Fallacy at work.

## What is the Base Rate Fallacy?

The Base Rate Fallacy is a cognitive bias that says that when it comes to making decisions, we put greater weight on specific information than we do on general information, even if the general information is more relevant. It was first studied by Maya Bar-Hillel in a 1986 study. Her conclusion was that people make snap judgments about the relevance of information that's presented to them, and use their arbitrary interpretation of relevance to drive their decisions.[1]

A later study dug a bit deeper to examine how and why we make use of statistical data. What it found is that we are hardwired to have a hard time interpreting statistics when we are presented with information that contradicts the data. For example, someone presented with a stadium full of Arab men dressed in robes might have a hard time evaluating a statistic that revealed that only one of the men was a terrorist.[2] The preconceived notion to think of Arabs as terrorists overrides the statistical probability of any one man actually being a terrorist.

Racial bias and the Base Rate Fallacy go hand in hand. A third study examined the connection between race and the Base Rate Fallacy in more depth. General conceptions about a person's ethnicity can make it difficult for some people to evaluate a person's qualities when statistical data is provided.[3] However, it is also true that on an individual basis the Base Rate Fallacy is far less common. When we know somebody, we don't make the same biased judgments about who they are.

## The Base Rate Fallacy in Marketing

When it comes to using the Base Rate Fallacy in marketing, they key is not to overestimate your customers' ability to evaluate and use statistical information in their decision-making process. Some customers may find such information useful, but for others it may prevent them from making a logical or correct decision.

Marketers can use the Base Rate Fallacy by using specific examples of how a product or service works instead of providing statistics. Statistics can work in combination with a case study or testimonial. Adding a personal touch to the data can make it easier for customers to overcome the Base Rate Fallacy.

**Examples of the Base Rate Fallacy in Action**

One interesting thing about using the Base Rate Fallacy in marketing is that marketers are just as susceptible to it as their target audience. The same techniques to use (and avoid) the Base Rate Fallacy can be used for both B2B and B2C marketing, so let's look at some examples.

1. Marketers who have a very technical product to promote, such as software, might be tempted to provide potential customers with a long list of information and usage statistics. The problem with doing that is that people don't respond as well to statistics as they do to stories. Instead, try featuring a case study of a person using your software. You can use some statistics to support the case study, but looking at one customer

will have a greater impact on buying decisions than presenting general statistics.

2. Consider producing a video that shows how your product works. People absorb data that's presented visually much more quickly than they do written information, and when you combine that with a personal story you've got a powerful one-two punch that can really help sell your product.

3. Putting three or four powerful customer testimonials on your website is more effective than telling people that your customer satisfaction rate is 95%. The number doesn't mean much to most people unless it's backed up by something specific. When you provide testimonials, your potential customers view those as proof that you're doing something right.

4. Use your social media accounts to tell stories. Story-telling is still one of the most powerful forms of marketing around, and social media is the perfect medium for it. You can use it to share testimonials or case studies, or to tell a story of how someone in your company helped a client out of a difficult situation.

5. Finally, don't fall victim to the Base Rate Fallacy yourself. There is such a thing is over-segmenting your

marketing. You might be tempted to spend a lot of effort marketing to a small group in spite of the fact that, statistically speaking, your ROI will be better with a large group, It's a fine line to walk, but don't let your preconceptions get in the way of running a successful marketing campaign.

We're all susceptible to the Base Rate Fallacy, but when you avoid generalizations and make your marketing specific, you can help your customers to get beyond it and buy your product.

## CITATIONS

1. Bar-Hillel, M. (1980). The base-rate fallacy in probability judgments. *Acta Psychologica, 44*(3), 211-233.
2. Allen, M., Preiss, R. W., & Gayle, B. M. (2006). Meta-analytic examination of the base-rate fallacy. *Communication Research Reports, 23*(1), 45-51.
3. Locksley, A., Hepburn, C., & Ortiz, V. (1982). Social stereotypes and judgments of individuals: An instance of the base-rate fallacy. *Journal of experimental social psychology, 18*(1), 23-42.

# CONFIRMATION BIAS:
# I KNOW WHAT I KNOW

Imagine that you are preparing to crack open a new video game. Your best friend recommended it to you and raved about how great it was. Not only that, but you've read a couple of reviews that talked about special features and Easter eggs. You're itching to get started. When you do, you find that the game and its features live up to your expectation.

What's wrong with that? Well, in this scenario let's say the game is actually only average. The features aren't particularly unique, and there are dozens of other games out there that are more entertaining. Why, you might be asking, would your experience be so out of synch with reality? It's because of a mental shortcut called the *Confirmation Bias*.

## Understanding the Confirmation Bias

The Confirmation Bias was first studied by British psychologist Peter Wason in 1960. In his study, he showed participants a series of numbers (2, 4, and 6) and asked them to provide a sequence of numbers that would match the criteria of the sequence he'd provided.[1] His explanation was quite simple – all he was looking for was a series of any three ascending numbers. Study participants, though, based their answers on their prior experiences and provided responses that reflected them. In other words, their answers confirmed what they already knew to be true.

Later studies looked at other iterations of the Confirmation Bias. One studied two groups of people who were given a particular food to taste.[2] One group was told beforehand that the food was healthy. The other group was given no information. The results showed that the first group, because of their negative associations with healthy food, found the item they ate to be less tasty and satisfying than the control group.

A third study examined how the Confirmation Bias affected both purchasing decisions and post-purchase use of the product.[3] It found that consumers' informational biases carried over to the way they used products after they bought them. If a consumer had a pre-conceived idea of how the product could be used, he would only use it in that way, even if information was available that indicated multiple uses for the product.

## The Confirmation Bias in Marketing

Marketers use many cognitive biases to sell their products, but the Confirmation Bias is one of the most common. Here are some ways you can use the Confirmation Bias in marketing:

1. Highlight a particular feature of your product or service that customers might not otherwise notice. In the absence of any effort to direct consumers' attention, you have no control over what they notice. However, if you make a point of talking about specific aspects of your product, you are ensuring that customers will notice it, and hopefully – after they buy it – have their advertising-induced opinions reinforced by the Confirmation Bias.

2. Describe the effect your product will have on your customers. Think of the healthy food example as a guideline. If participants had been told that the food

was highly rated and that previous study participants had proclaimed it to be delicious, they would have had a very different response to it. Find subtle ways to tell your customers what to expect from your product, and you increase the chances that their expectations will be met.

## Examples of the Confirmation Bias at Work

The Confirmation Bias is a powerful tool for any marketer to use. Let's look at some examples from B2B marketing:

1.  A company looking for a new way to market business products might choose to change its marketing focus from the products themselves to their customer service. They could run a marketing campaign featuring stories of customers explaining how happy they were with the customer service they received. They might also put their customer service team in videos or feature them in pictures. Putting the spotlight on customer service makes it more likely that clients will notice it, even if they normally take it for granted.
2.  This same tactic can work for a pricing process. A lot

of companies use boilerplate pricing. A company that tailored prices to each individual client might decide to talk about their pricing process in a campaign. The focus on pricing could actually help the sales team justify the prices being charged because the client believes that serious effort and evaluation have gone into the quote they received.

The Confirmation Bias is equally effective in B2C marketing:

1. A while back, Holiday Inn installed new showerheads in their hotel. Most hotel guests probably never notice the showerhead, as long as it's clean, and it works. They called their showerheads the "Stay Smart Showerhead" and left information in the guestrooms about the benefits of using it. Guests who stayed there felt they were getting something special, and it increased their enjoyment of their stay and their positive opinion of Holiday Inn.

2. Advertising pioneer Claude Hopkins used the Confirmation Bias in a campaign he created for Schlitz Beer. At the time he toured Schlitz's plant, they were fifth in the market – not very impressive. He noted the elaborate purification process they used

to manufacture the beer, and decided to highlight the process – and the beer's purity – in its advertising. As a result, Schlitz took over the number one spot in the beer market.

As you can see, the Confirmation Bias is a powerful way to focus your clients' attention on particular features, and to make it more likely that they'll have a positive experience with your product or brand. It's hard to change people's minds, but it's very easy to confirm what they already know – you just have to tell them what you want them to know first.

## CITATIONS

1. Wason, P. C. (1960). On the failure to eliminate hypotheses in a conceptual task. *Quarterly journal of experimental psychology, 12*(3), 129-140.
2. Raghunathan, R., Naylor, R. W., & Hoyer, W. D. (2006). The unhealthy= tasty intuition and its effects on taste inferences, enjoyment, and choice of food products. *Journal of Marketing, 70*(4), 170-184.
3. Jones, M., & Sugden, R. (2001). Positive confirmation bias in the acquisition of information. *Theory and Decision, 50*(1), 59-99.

# DISTINCTION BIAS:
# LESS IS MORE

Imagine that you are walking down the street, and you pass a bakery. The aroma is enticing, and you decide to go in and get yourself a treat. When you walk up to the case, you see that there is a single chocolate chip cookie left. You buy it, you eat it, and you enjoy it thoroughly. Sounds great, right?

Now imagine that you walk into the same bakery, and there are two cookies. They're both chocolate chip cookies, and you know you like chocolate chips, so you would probably enjoy either one. However, there are differences, and you can't help making comparisons. That one's a little bigger, so maybe it's a better value – but the other one looks like it has more chocolate chips, and they're the best part of the cookie. You end up choosing the first one – the bigger one – and you enjoy it. But when you're done, some part of you wonders if you shouldn't have chosen the second one, even though in the first scenario you thoroughly enjoyed the first cookie and had no regrets.

What's going on? Why is choosing between two cookies such a big deal? It's because of a mental shortcut called the Distinction Bias, and we all fall victim to it sometimes.

## Understanding Distinction Bias

Human beings are predisposed to prefer joint evaluations. We like to make comparisons, and we prefer situations where we can do so easily. However, doing a side-by-side evaluation can actually make us overestimate the differences between things. A 2004 study by Christopher Hsee and Jiao Zhang examined the way we evaluate things like getting a salary increase by changing jobs.[1] The salary itself might be the only real difference, and yet we tend to put a larger emphasis on it because we are looking at it side by side. A person who's unhappy with his job might end up switching, only to discover that he's in the same boat except for the salary.

A 2009 study about diversity in hiring decisions found that side by side comparisons actually helped employers be more diverse in their decision-making because evaluating candidates simultaneously highlighted their differences.[2]

When diversity is the goal, the Distinction Bias becomes an advantage.

Finally, a 2007 study about hedonics and consumer behavior showed that avoiding the Distinction Bias (in other words, making fewer comparisons) increased consumer happiness after the purchase.[3]

## Distinction Bias in Marketing

Some marketers seem to think that more choices are necessarily better for consumers, but that's not always the case. We've all been in a situation where we go to a restaurant with a huge menu and find that we're paralyzed by the number of options. If you sell a lot of similar products with minor differences, it may actually be helpful to avoid side-by-side comparisons of their features. Consumers may get bogged down in minor details and be unable to make a decision.

The opposite approach can be helpful if you want to draw distinctions between your company and a competitor. The differences may actually be small, but if you put your product side by side with theirs, consumers will see the differences as being larger than they are. That can be a helpful marketing tool in a competitive environment.

**Examples of the Distinction Bias in Action**

The Distinction Bias can work in both B2B and B2C marketing. Let's look at some examples, starting with B2B:

1. Presenting a potential client with too many choices is a mistake. Instead, highlight the things you want them to notice. For example, let's say that your technical support differs from your competitor's in some important ways. Instead of giving clients a bullet list that lets them compare every feature of your services, focus on the one that you think is your biggest selling point. "Our customer service is available by phone or online 24 hours a day, but our competitor's is only available online, and it may take two days for them to get back to you." Drawing a distinction like that gives your customers something valuable and relevant to focus on without getting distracted by other, less relevant features.

2. When offering options for service package, limit the number of choices you provide. In general, offering two, three, or four choices is fine – any more than that, and you run the risk of paralyzing people with too much information.

Now let's look at some B2C marketing examples:

1. Retailers who carry a wide range of products sometimes go overboard with comparisons. If you sell six different laptop computers, don't offer customers a chart comparing all six of them. That's too much information for them to process. Instead, focus on one or two features and compare computers that are close in price. Most customers who come in will have a price range in mind, and there's no need to show them the computers they have no intention of buying.

2. Understand what's most important to your customers, and focus your advertising on those features. For example, if you are selling an environmentally-friendly product, you might know that your customers are interested in products that will protect natural resources. Instead of giving them a huge list of

information, focus on the few features that are most important to them. You don't need to give them a laundry list of everything your product can do.

The key to using the Distinction Bias is to work with the information you have about your clients and use it to help steer them in the direction you want them to go. Everyone struggles with decision making, and it's your job to smooth the rough edges and make it easier for customers to focus on the things that are most important to them. Not only will doing so increase your sales, it will also increase customer satisfaction because they are less likely to make decisions based on irrelevant data.

## CITATIONS

1. Hsee, C. K., & Zhang, J. (2004). Distinction bias: misprediction and mischoice due to joint evaluation. *Journal of personality and social psychology*, *86*(5), 680.
2. Brooks, M. E., Guidroz, A. M., & Chakrabarti, M. (2009). Distinction bias in applicant reactions to using diversity information in selection. *International Journal of Selection and Assessment*, *17*(4), 377-390.

3. Hsee, C. K., & Tsai, C. I. (2007). Hedonics in Consumer Behavior. *HANDBOOK OF CONSUMER PSYCHOLOGY, CP Haugtvedt, PM Herr, and FR Kardes, eds*, 639-658.

# GOOD MONEY AFTER BAD:
# THE IRRATIONAL ESCALATION BIAS

You're on vacation, and you're fortunate enough to have been able to afford a beach holiday. You bring a book down to the beach and start to read it. By the time you get a hundred pages in, you're fed up with it. It's badly written, and you don't like the characters, but you've already invested a couple of hours reading it. In spite of the fact that you're not enjoying the book, you keep reading because, as you tell yourself, you've already wasted this much time, and you might as well finish it.

On the surface, the decision to keep reading makes no sense. You've already spent the money on the book, and if you know won't enjoy reading the rest of it there's no point in continuing. All you will do is waste more time. Despite its lack of logic, this type of decision is one we all make frequently. It's the result of a cognitive bias called the *Irrational Escalation Bias*.

## What is the Irrational Escalation Bias?

The Irrational Escalation Bias is a mental shortcut first identified by researcher Barry Staw in 1976. In his study, he discovered that when participants experienced a negative outcome as the result of an action, they were likely to continue along that same course of action in the expectation that eventually, their luck would change.[1] This particular bias can apply to something as simple as reading a bad book, as mentioned above, or as complex as a military operation. People tend to attach value to their previous actions, and they are reluctant to abandon them in favor of a new tactic even when they are not proving to be effective.

Staw did a follow-up study that investigated the reason behind the Irrational Escalation Bias, which is also sometimes referred to as the *Sunk Cost Bias*. His additional research revealed that people tend to believe they can recoup their losses by continuing on the same course, even in the presence of evidence that suggests the opposite.[2] The book example above is a good illustration of this. If a book is badly written, it's highly improbable that the quality of the writing – or your enjoyment of it – will change as you read more. A far more likely outcome is that you'll continue to be annoyed and wish that you'd stopped reading when you had the chance.

Another way the Irrational Escalation Bias can play out is in auctions. A certain percentage of bidders enter an auction with a spending cap in mind. The Irrational Escalation Bias can make them continue to bid more than they intended because they believe that having the item will somehow make up for the additional expense.[3]

## The Irrational Escalation Bias in Marketing

Like many other cognitive biases, the Irrational Escalation Bias can be a useful marketing tool. For example, an internet marketer might sell customers a low-priced product with minimal features when they first enter his sales funnel. He can then leverage that small initial investment by framing it as a sunk cost. Once the customer has made the initial purchase, she's more likely to double down and make a second one, even if she's received no tangible benefits from the first product she bought.

The same principle holds for business services. The more a client has put into a particular course of action, the easier it will be to convince them to continue with it. For example, you might remind a customer of her initial investment as a way of getting her to escalate her involvement with your company. Charities use this strategy all the time.

## The Irrational Escalation Bias in Action

Let's look at a few examples of the Irrational Escalation Bias as it's used in marketing campaigns, starting with B2B marketing:

1. A financial services company charges a monthly fee and promises to earn their clients a certain result. If the customer hasn't attained the goals they hoped for, they might start shopping around for another company. One way their existent company can prevent that from happening is by reminding their client how much money they have already invested in the current strategy. The services offered by the competing company don't even need to be compatible for this strategy to work. Obviously you want to be careful about constantly reminding customers about how much your services cost, but if you refer to the costs as an investment it can be very effective.

2. Consider using a "foot in the door" strategy with new customers. Start them off with a basic service, and then after they've been using it for a while, you can market a more costly option to them framing the additional costs as an investment in their company. A subtle reminder of what they've already invested can be enough to get them to upgrade.

The Irrational Escalation bias has its place in B2C marketing, as well:

1. After customers have made a purchase, they often seek confirmation that the choice they made was a wise one. One way to use that information to your advantage is to remind them of the wisdom of their choices. For example, a weight loss service might use phrases like, "You've already made a smart decision by joining" in their marketing materials. Language like that helps customers to avoid cognitive dissonance and makes it easier for them to purchase additional services.

2. The "foot in the door" strategy can work for B2C marketing too. Instead of trying to sell a customer on something big, start small and work your way up. A

customer who's already made the decision to buy from you is more likely to buy again.

As you can see, the Irrational Escalation Bias can be a very powerful tool for marketers, especially when it is used for client retention and repeated sales. Nobody likes to feel they've made a bad decision, so do everything you can to remind your clients that their choices are good.

## CITATIONS

1. Staw, B. M. (1976). Knee-deep in the big muddy: A study of escalating commitment to a chosen course of action. *Organizational behavior and human performance*, *16*(1), 27-44.
2. Staw, B. M. (1981). The escalation of commitment to a course of action. *Academy of management Review*, *6*(4), 577-587.
3. Park, S. C., Kim, J. U., & Bock, G. W. (2008). Understanding a bidder's escalation of commitment in the online C2C auction. In *European Mediterranean Conference on Information Systems (EMCIS)*.

# HAPPILY EVER AFTER: THE IMPACT BIAS

Imagine that you're out car shopping. You've been driving an old car. It gets you around, but it's nothing special. However, you've been working hard and saving money, and at long last, you have enough to buy the luxury car you've always wanted. You go into the dealership and take the car you want for a test drive. As you sink into its soft leather seats and inhale the new car smell, you allow yourself a moment to think ahead to how happy owning this car is going to make you. It's going to make everything in your life better. You just know it.

That's an awful lot of pressure to put on a car, but that kind of thinking is surprisingly common. It's a cognitive bias called the *Impact Bias.*

## What is the Impact Bias?

The Impact Bias says that people, in general, have a tendency to overestimate the impact that events in the present will have on their future selves. It was first named in a 2002 study by Daniel Gilbert, Erin Driver-Linn and Timothy Wilson, who explored the way humans predict and remember events.[1] Our imaginations, it turns out, are rather limited when it comes to making predictions about how things will affect us.

The same researchers followed up with a study in 2003 that examined the way we discuss the impact of past events.[2] The Impact Bias works in reverse, too – we overestimate the impact that past events had on us. The example used in the study was of the 2000 Gore/Bush election in the United States. Part of the reason that the Impact Bias is so powerful is that we tend to focus on a single event to the exclusion of all others.

The Impact Bias comes into play in multiple areas of our lives. For example, people who are engaged in negotiations tend to "miswant" because of their inability to predict the impact of the current negotiations on their future selves.[3] The Impact Bias leads people to dig their heels in about things that end up not being very important and to miss opportunities that might make a big difference.

## The Impact Bias in Marketing

The Impact Bias is very popular in advertising campaigns. Because people already have a tendency to overestimate the effects of their current actions on their future selves, advertisers regularly present pictures of ecstatic customers using their products. One classic example involves beer commercials. The people drinking beer in those ads are always beautiful and happy. They're part of a big party, and everybody's having the time of their lives. Drinking a beer or two is not going to land you in the middle of the party of the century, surrounded by models.

Because the Impact Bias works both ways (for predicting the past and remembering the future) it's a very versatile tool for marketers to use. You can take advantage of the way customers see the past by exaggerating the misery they had felt before they had your product.

## The Impact Bias in Action

Now that you understand how the Impact Bias can work in marketing, let's take a look at a few examples, starting with B2C marketing:

1. If you've ever been awake watching late-night television, you've seen an infomercial. Especially when they're advertising kitchen gadgets, they tend to use the Impact Bias to convince viewers to buy their products. There's one for a pasta pot with a built-in strainer. The commercial shows a woman pouring pasta into a colander and losing half of it down the sink. Very few people are that sloppy, but a person watching it might, because of the Impact Bias, decide that their past pasta-draining experiences were worse than they actually were. If that happens, they'll be far more likely to go online and order the pasta drainer.

2. Weight Watchers uses the Impact Bias all the time in their commercials. Because they feature impossibly slim celebrity spokespeople, they are encouraging people to think, if I sign up for Weight Watchers, I'll end up looking like Jennifer Hudson! Clearly that's not the case – even if you lose a lot of weight, you won't be Jennifer Hudson. The subliminal message is a strong one, and it's effective. That's the Impact Bias at work.

The Impact Bias also has applications in B2B marketing:

1. Marketers who are selling business services can emphasize the amount of happiness and satisfaction clients will feel if they sign on. There are a number of ways to do that. You should obviously avoid making specific predictions about the future, but when you keep potential clients focused on how they'll feel in the future, you can take advantage of the Impact Bias. Some examples of how to use the Impact Bias include sharing customer testimonials or even sharing a success story that emphasizes the impact of your product.

2. You can do the same thing by putting your client's focus on past problems. When dealing with a lead, you can use the information they've confided in you about past problems to take advantage of the Impact Bias. For example, say you're offering business consulting services and you know from looking at a potential client's financials that they had some tax trouble in the past. You could play up how horrible that was and then point to how much better it will be if they sign on with you. If many of your clients come in with the

same past problems, you can use those in marketing campaigns.

The Impact Bias is very powerful and difficult for people to overcome. When you understand how it works, you can use it to get customers to focus on the rosy future they can expect if they buy your product or sign up for your service. Once you have them on board, you can continue to use it to help you retain clients.

## CITATIONS

1. Gilbert, D. T., Driver-Linn, E., & Wilson, T. D. (2002). The trouble with Vronsky: Impact bias in the forecasting of future affective states.
2. Wilson, T. D., Meyers, J., & Gilbert, D. T. (2003). "How happy was I, anyway?" A retrospective impact bias. *Social Cognition*, *21*(6), 421-446.
3. Guthrie, C., & Sally, D. F. (2004). The impact of the impact bias on negotiation. *Marquette Law Review*, *87*

# HYPERBOLIC DISCOUNTING: GIVE IT TO ME NOW

In the movie *Postcards from the Edge*, the Meryl Streep character says, "Instant gratification takes too long." It sounds like a joke, but the truth is that, as a species, we are hardwired to value immediate rewards over long-term ones.

Imagine that you're walking down the street, and you run into your uncle. He says, "I have two fifty dollar bills in my pocket. You have a choice. I can give you one of them right now, and you'll have fifty bucks you didn't have before. Or, you can meet me back here next week, and I'll give them both to you." If you're like most people, you would choose the fifty dollars now instead of waiting to see if he actually showed up the following week.

On the surface, that might not seem to make sense. Why not take a chance and wait for the hundred dollar reward? After all, a hundred dollars is objectively better than fifty dollars, right? The reason most people would take the first offer is due to a cognitive bias known as *Hyperbolic Discounting*.

## What is Hyperbolic Discounting?

The concept of Hyperbolic Discounting was first studied by researcher George Ainslie in 1974. His study involved getting pigeons to peck a button. If they pecked the button, they were rewarded with a small piece of food. If they resisted the urge to peck the button and get the reward, they were given a larger reward. Despite the clear advantage of waiting, 95% of the pigeons pecked the button.[1] The results changed slightly when a button of a different color was introduced. Pecking this button eliminated the option of getting a treat from the other button. In the new circumstance, 30% of the pigeons chose to peck the new button, thus forcing themselves to wait for the larger reward.

Hyperbolic Discounting also plays a big role in our ability to save money for future events. Two studies have examined this phenomenon. The first study focused on the way financial innovations have altered our ability to save money. Specifically, it looked at the ways in which credit cards enable our tendency toward Hyperbolic Discounting.[2] As a rule, we don't look at the fact that charging a purchase means that we'll end up paying more for it when interest rates are taken into account.

The second study examined the way people save for retirement. Instead of merely looking at what was saved, the study also asked retirees what they thought about their preparations for retirement. A large majority said that they thought their younger selves should have worked longer and saved more.[3]

The Hyperbolic Discount is powerful, and it often leads us to make decisions that our future selves will regret.

## Hyperbolic Discounting in Marketing

In a lot of ways, the Hyperbolic Discount is a cognitive bias that's made for marketers. The propensity of consumers to want things now is strong, and easy to use to your advantage. One way to use it is to offer the chance to delay making payments – let the customer use your product now and pay for it later.

An alternative use of Hyperbolic Discount is to give customers a gift with their purchase. The free gift satisfies their need for immediate gratification and makes it easier for them to make the purchase. You can also entice customers to sign up for a short-term subscription at a lower price – even if signing up for the long-term subscription makes more financial sense.

## Examples of Hyperbolic Discounting

A lot of marketers use Hyperbolic Discounting without understanding why it works. Here are some examples, starting with B2C marketing:

1. Furniture stores frequently offer customers a "Buy now, pay nothing until next year" option. Logically, it makes more sense to pay for the furniture now, so you don't have to pay finance fees, but letting customers have the furniture now triggers Hyperbolic Discounting and consumers think they're getting a better deal.

2. The same lack of logic applies to store credit cards. Department stores offer customers the opportunity to apply at the counter and get a discount off their purchase – usually 10% or so. The store does it because they now the amount of the discount will be eclipsed by what the customer will end up paying in interest. The customer's focus is on the immediate gratification of the discount, and they don't stop to think about it what it will cost them in the long run.

Hyperbolic Discounting works in B2B marketing too. Let's look at a few examples:

1. A company that offers clients a subscription or membership service might have difficulty convincing clients to pay $49.99 for a full-year subscription, because it's asking them to pay up front for something they won't get until later. A clever marketer can flip this on its ear by offering a shorter-term subscription for less money – for example, asking a client to pay $9.99 a month for a subscription. Objectively speaking, that makes no sense. Twelve months at $9.99 per month is $119.88, more than twice the cost of the full-year subscription. However nonsensical it might seem, most clients won't stop to do the math.

2. Giving out a free gift is another way of triggering Hyperbolic Discounting. A lot of business service companies offer potential clients a free month of membership or a free product. For example, a company that sells copy machines might offer free paper with purchase. The value of the paper is completely eclipsed by the cost of the machine, but the client's focus is on the immediate gratification of getting the free paper.

As you can see, Hyperbolic Discounting is a powerful tool for marketers. If you use it properly, you may be able to charge more for your product and still make clients believe they're getting a bargain.

## CITATIONS

1. Ainslie, G. W. (1974). Impulse control in pigeons. *Journal of the experimental analysis of behavior, 21*(3), 485.
2. Laibson, D. (1997). Golden eggs and hyperbolic discounting. *The Quarterly Journal of Economics*, 443-477.
3. Diamond, P., & Köszegi, B. (2003). Quasi-hyperbolic discounting and retirement. *Journal of Public Economics, 87*(9), 1839-1872.

# I MADE IT MYSELF:
# THE IKEA EFFECT

I magine you're at a pot-luck dinner hosted by a friend. You worked for hours that day to make veggie lasagna – your specialty. When you arrived and unwrapped your lasagna, you noticed that someone else had brought a veggie lasagna too. It looked beautiful, and it was clearly homemade. As you worked your way down the buffet line, you took a piece of your lasagna and a smaller one of the other one, just to compare. Not surprisingly, you preferred the one you made.[1]

Yours may have been objectively better than the other lasagna, or it may not have been. If most of the other guests preferred the second lasagna, though, chances are good that you experienced a cognitive bias called the *IKEA Effect*.

## Understanding the IKEA Effect

As you might have guessed, the IKEA Effect is named after the popular IKEA stores. If you've ever been to one, you know that the furniture they sell is not fully assembled. After you buy it, you have to take it home and complete the assembly yourself. Researchers Michael Norton, Daniel Mochon and Dan Ariely first identified the IKEA Effect in 2011.[2] What it says is that people place a higher value on items they have built or partially built themselves than on items built by others, even in cases where the "other" is a master craftsman. In other words, labor equals love.

In a follow-up study, the same three researchers dug deeper into the topic. They found that the reason that study participants valued self-assembled work more highly was that it allowed them to restore and bolster their feelings of competence[3] to themselves and others. Individuals who already felt they were highly competent were not as biased as those whose competence needed a lift.

## The IKEA Effect in Marketing

The most obvious example of the IKEA Effect in marketing is IKEA itself. The store is very popular, and people have been known to drive hundreds of miles just to shop there. Clearly their business model is working. However, do-it-yourself products are hardly new. For years, retailers like Sears and Target have been selling furniture that requires partial assembly at home.

In general, the way marketers can you the IKEA Effect to their advantage is to find a way to give consumers or clients a sense of ownership in the product that goes beyond having paid for it. When people feel that their own sweat, whether literal or figurative, has gone into a product, they feel a sense of pride and ownership that they would not feel, otherwise. That same feeling can translate into brand loyalty because they feel they are "in it" with the brand.

**Examples of the IKEA Effect in Use**

At first glance, it might seem as though the IKEA Effect only lends itself to B2C marketing. After all, how can a B2B marketer – especially one who's marketing something intangible, like a service – give clients the feeling that they've done that service themselves? Let's look at one possibility:

Accounts receivable factoring companies use software to manage their clients' accounts. They keep track of invoice aging reports and credit for their clients' customers, among other things. How, you might wonder, could such a company give clients a sense of ownership? In the past several years, one of the companies that make factoring software has added a feature that allows clients to access the software online through a separate portal. They can then run ad hoc reports, track progress, and ask questions as needed. In other words, it gives them a "do-it-yourself" feeling that makes them feel they have a greater sense of control.

That same idea could be adapted for any number of B2B companies.

Another example in B2B marketing is used by investment companies. Customers have the ability to move their investments around and reallocate them. Not only does this give them a sense of ownership, it probably decreases the chances that the investment company will take the brunt of the blame if a client's investment goes wrong.

Examples of the IKEA Effect in B2C marketing are very common. Let's look at a few:

1. The popular company Build-a-Bear lets children pick the components of a teddy bear and participate in its assembly. Kids get to pick the color of their bear, what it's wearing, and even how firmly it's stuffed. They participate further by placing a plastic heart inside the bear. The company can charge significantly more than they could for a pre-assembled bear because the experience of building the bear increases its value to customers.

2. Another similar example is do-it-yourself pottery stores. Customers pay for a plain piece of pottery – a plate or a jug – and then they use paints that the store provides to decorate them. Unless the customer is a professional artist, chances are good that the finished product will be objectively less attractive than one decorated by a pro, but the act of decorating it adds to its perceived worth. Here again, the IKEA Effect is both about attracting customers by adding an assembly experience to the purchasing process, and about increasing profit margins.

3. The IKEA Effect can apply to restaurants and food service as well. When restaurants let customers build their own pizza or assemble the ingredients for a

stir-fry, they're letting them feel like the made the food themselves.

When it's used properly, the IKEA Effect can accomplish two things. First, it can attract customers who enjoy a hands-on approach and who feel the need to boost their competence – even if they're not consciously aware of it. And second, it can allow businesses to charge more because the customer's labor and the experience involved with the purchase increase the perceived value of the product being sold.

## CITATIONS

1. Dohle, S., Rall, S., & Siegrist, M. (2014). I cooked it myself: Preparing food increases liking and consumption. *Food Quality and Preference*, *33*, 14-16.
2. Norton, M. I., Mochon, D., & Ariely, D. (2011). The'IKEA effect': When labor leads to love. *Harvard Business School Marketing Unit Working Paper*, (11-091).
3. Mochon, D., Norton, M. I., & Ariely, D. (2012). Bolstering and restoring feelings of competence via the IKEA effect. *International Journal of Research in Marketing*, *29*(4), 363-369.

# FREE RESOURCES FROM SAM PAGE AND THE NEURO TRIGGERS TEAM

As an expression of gratitude for reading this book, I would like to offer you two FREE gifts so you can leverage the power of marketing psychology in your own business.

- **Visual Impact Map.** How well does your website engage your users' reptilian brain? Using predictive analysis, we'll present a full color map outlining your website's primary engagement points. *(Normally $129).*
- **Follow-up consultation and discovery session** (with a licensed consumer psychologist) to review your neuromarketing score. *(Normally $250).*

To claim these FREE gifts, just head on over to our website at
www.NeuroTriggersAgency.com or shoot us an email at
support@NeuroTriggersAgency.com.

# LOSS AVERSION:
# DON'T TAKE WHAT BELONGS TO ME

Imagine you're at work, and you overhear your boss on the phone. He's telling someone that he's getting ready to do performance reviews and that you'll be getting a $250 weekly raise. That's exciting, right? You want to get the raise, and you probably start thinking about how you could spend the extra money.

Now imagine the flip side of that situation. You overhear your boss on the phone, but this time he's talking about the fact that the company's struggling and he's going to have to cut costs. One of the ways he's going to do that is by cutting your pay by $250 a week.

If you're like most people, your reaction to the second scenario would be far stronger than your reaction to the first. You would probably feel high levels of anger and fear at the thought of losing some of your weekly paycheck – much higher than the corresponding joy at the thought of an increase. The reason for this is a cognitive bias called *Loss Aversion*.

## Understanding Loss Aversion

The principle of Loss Aversion says that, as a rule, we place a higher premium on things we already own than things we don't. Researchers Amos Tversky and Daniel Kahneman first identified this particular cognitive bias in their 1991 study, Loss Aversion in Riskless Choice.[1] In the study, they looked at participants who were registering for a conference. One group was offered the opportunity to save five dollars if they registered early. The choice was framed as an early registration discount. The second group was offered a regular registration price – the same as the early registration price presented to the other group – but told they'd be charged a five dollar penalty if they registered late. Participants in the second group were far more likely to register early because they viewed the late fee as a five dollar loss.

Another example of the way Loss Aversion works was illustrated in a 1993 study about changes in product features.[2] In this study, participants were presented with the possibility of products being reformulated so they lost particular features. What the study revealed was that consumers took it personally if brands changed formulas or features, because they felt ownership of those features. Loss Aversion probably explains why the new Coke formula was such a disaster. Consumers felt that they owned the old Coke formula, and they reacted strongly to the idea of it being taken from them.

Let's look at one final aspect of Loss Aversion before we talk about some examples. A 2000 study showed that participants were more averse to loss when they owned hedonic goods than when they owned utilitarian ones.[3] For example, the owner of a luxury car reacted more angrily to the idea of losing it than the owner of a basic model car reacted to the same thought. The higher the perceived value of the item in question, the stronger the cognitive bias becomes.

## Loss Aversion in Marketing

The key to using Loss Aversion in marketing is to instill a sense of ownership in your potential customers even before they make a purchase. That sounds tricky, but let's look at an example. Monster internet retailer Amazon sells a Prime service that offers members some desirable perks, including free 2-day shipping and access to free streaming videos. The service costs $99 for one year. Amazon gets customers to sign up for a one-month free trial, during which time they can take advantage of all of the perks they'd get if they joined the service. The free trial makes customers feel that they already own those services. The sense of ownership they get from the free trial makes it far more likely that they'll continue and pay the membership fee when the trial comes to a close, because they don't want to lose what they already have.

**Examples of Loss Aversion in Action**

Now let's take a look at some of the ways marketers can use Loss Aversion to their advantage, starting with B2B:

1. We already talked about free trial memberships, but free consultations can work the same way. The owner of a business consulting firm might offer a free, one-hour consultation to potential clients. By offering a taste of what the client could have – and by framing the choice in the right way, pointing out what the potential client has to lose if they don't sign on – the firm can greatly increase the chances that the client will sign on the dotted line.

2. Another alternative is to make a video showing a client using your product. As a rule, potential clients will identify with the people they see in your video. You can increase their sense of attachment to the

product by saying things like "Imagine yourself here" or "This could be you." Those phrases build up a sense of ownership.

Loss Aversion is also common in B2C marketing. For example:

1. Some companies offer free samples of their products. A good example of this is cosmetics retailer Sephora. Every customer who places an order online gets to choose three free samples. Letting customers choose ensures that they'll get samples that appeal to them, and Sephora knows that letting customers have a small amount of something for free increases the chances that they'll buy it later.

2. B2C marketers can use loss aversion in a more subtle way by framing their advertising in a way that emphasizes loss. You've probably seen those infomercials selling food dehydrators. The way they are framed focuses on the amount of money customers are losing by not buying the product. Buying the product will require an expenditure, but the goal is to make them look at spending as a gain instead of as a loss.

Loss Aversion is one of the most powerful cognitive biases we have. The key to using it well is to frame the information you are presenting properly. If you can make customers feel that spending money is a gain instead of a loss, then Loss Aversion can work for you.

## CITATIONS

1. Tversky, A., & Kahneman, D. (1991). Loss aversion in riskless choice: A reference-dependent model. *The quarterly journal of economics*, 1039-1061.
2. Hardie, B. G., Johnson, E. J., & Fader, P. S. (1993). Modeling loss aversion and reference dependence effects on brand choice. *Marketing science*, *12*(4), 378-394.
3. Dhar, R., & Wertenbroch, K. (2000). Consumer choice between hedonic and utilitarian goods. *Journal of marketing research*, *37*(1), 60-71.

# MORE IS BETTER (EVEN WHEN IT'S NOT): THE INFORMATION BIAS

I magine that you're on a website, and you're trying to choose between two different computers. Both are in your price range. Both have similar features. The only perceptible difference is that one computer has a long description with lots of information included, while the other has only a few relevant bullet points describing it. Even if the information included with the first computer is not relevant to your particular needs, you are still more likely to buy it than the second one.

Why is more information better than less? Why does relevance not seem to play a part in your decision? It's because of a cognitive bias known as the *Information Bias*.

## What is the Information Bias?

The Information Bias was first identified by researchers Jonathan Barron, Jane Beattie and John Hershey in their 1988 study, *Congruence, Information and Certainty*.[1] In the study, they asked participants to evaluate options for medical testing in a hypothetical situation where 80% of a population has a particular disease. Participants were given detailed information about a possible test that had a 50% chance of returning a false result (either positive or negative) in people who had the disease. It was more accurate at detecting other, less-common diseases. The test was expensive, and the inaccuracy of the test in question meant that, regardless of the results, the people who were tested would need to be treated for the most probable disease.

The inaccuracy of the test and its expense were not enough to trump the Information Bias in the study's participants. They overwhelmingly said they would administer the test, even though doing so would not change the recommended course of action.

As with most cognitive biases, the participants' responses seem to fly in the face of reason. Why spend money on a test that will objectively do no good, and offer no guidance in terms of providing treatment? The faulty perception is that more information is good, and the quality of the information makes little difference in the decision-making process.

## The Information Bias in Marketing

There are several different ways marketers can take advantage of the Information Bias in their campaigns. Let's start with the most obvious. Providing a high volume of information about your product or service can make it easier for potential customers to dismiss any objections they might have to buying from you. The information may or may not be relevant in terms of content. The basic tenet of this bias is that more is better.

Another thing to keep in mind is that there does seem to be a tendency to place more weight on information that's perceived as being objective. For example, a 2005 study of customer behavior when purchasing wine showed that customers gave more weight to information from sources like wine magazines and well-known reviewers than they did to information they got from friends or the person selling the wine.[2] The lesson here is that the source of the information does matter, even if the quality of it does not. Marketers can take advantage of this by providing endorsements from experts.

One final point of interest regarding the Information Bias is this: tacit information and explicit information were equally important when it came to buying decisions.[3] Tacit information is information that is difficult to convey in words. For example, you can give someone a recipe to make a loaf of French bread, but it's extremely difficult to explain to them the way they dough should feel when it's ready. The only way to learn that is through experience. In terms of marketing, tacit information is not a useful thing because it will vary from person to person. However, if you're selling a product where your customer is likely to possess tacit information, providing a large amount of explicit information may help to sell your product.

**Examples of the Information Bias at Work**

Let's take a look at some of the ways the Information Bias can work in marketing, starting with some B2B examples:

1. If you are marketing a B2B service, it may be better to use long-form web pages than to use short ones. There's a tendency among some marketers to think that less is more, but when it comes to the Information

Bias, the opposite is true. People also tend to retain information better if they have to spend more time reading it. Consider adding as much information as you can to your marketing materials.

2. Consider using an opinion or endorsement of your product that can be seen as objective. Examples might include a quote from an industry influencer or information from a government report that supports one of your claims. Your potential clients will give the information they see as objective greater weight than information they see as subjective. That doesn't mean you shouldn't make claims about what you can do, but bolster them with something objective as well.

The Information Bias can work in B2C marketing, too:

1. Whether you are listing a product in your store or online, include as much information as possible about its features and benefits. When you include facts and figures, as well as detailed descriptions, you make it more likely that customers will pull the trigger and buy it. Remember, not all of the information needs to be hyper-relevant. For example, chances are someone

buying a computer doesn't care about every kind of software that comes installed on it, but if you list all of them you make it seem like a better value.

2. Restaurants sometimes go to great lengths to include information about their ingredients in the descriptions on their menus. For example, they might tell you were the radishes in your salad were grown, and what variety they are. A good marketing strategy would be to include extra information about specials because their goal is to sell as many of them as possible. When the restaurant provides more information, they increase the chances that you'll choose the special.

As you can see, the Information Bias can be a powerful marketing tool. The key to using it is to provide a high volume of information, take your customers' implicit information into account whenever possible, and include objective information if it's available.

## CITATIONS

1. Baron, J., Beattie, J., & Hershey, J. C. (1988). Heuristics and biases in diagnostic reasoning: II. Congruence,

information, and certainty. *Organizational Behavior and Human Decision Processes, 42*(1), 88-110.

2. Dodd, T. H., Laverie, D. A., Wilcox, J. F., & Duhan, D. F. (2005). Differential effects of experience, subjective knowledge, and objective knowledge on sources of information used in consumer wine purchasing. *Journal of Hospitality & Tourism Research, 29*(1), 3-19.

3. Giunipero, L., Dawley, D., & Anthony, W. P. (1999). The impact of tacit knowledge on purchasing decisions. *Journal of supply chain Management, 35*(4), 42-49.

# NEGATIVITY BIAS:
# WHEN BAD IS GOOD

Imagine that you're shopping for a new television. You're at a big box store, and you ask a salesperson to help you. She asks your price range and walks you through your options. There are a lot of choices, and it's a little overwhelming. Finally, you ask her which TV she'd buy, and she tells you. The only problem is, you know two people who've had that brand of television before, and they both had bad things to say about it. Admittedly, that was a long time ago, and you've heard more positive things since, but you can't quite shake the feeling, and you end up going with another option.

Sound familiar? It should. It's a cognitive bias called the Negativity Bias, and it's something we're all susceptible to.

**What is the Negativity Bias?**

The Negativity Bias is one of the most powerful cognitive biases, and it's one we all share – even though we might like to believe we don't. What it says is that, all things being equal, we do a better job of remembering negative experiences than we do positive ones. The Negativity Bias was first identified by researchers Paul Rosin and Edward Royzman.[1] They studied the different ways in which we react to negative and positive stimuli. Their research revealed that we perceive negative entities to be stronger than positive ones and that negative reactions tend to accelerate more than positive ones.

A later study studied how quickly the Negativity Bias affects us, and discovered that we see images or information and sort them into negative, positive and neutral categories immediately.[2] As soon as the sorting is finished, the Negativity Bias takes effect and begins to influence the way we process what we have seen.

One interesting corollary to the Negativity Bias was revealed in a 1998 study. It showed that the brain responds equally to negative information whether it is presented as a picture or as text. However, when a negative picture and negative text were presented together, they actually seemed to cancel each other out and produce the opposite result.[3]

## The Negativity Bias in Marketing

The Negativity Bias can be a little nerve-wracking for marketers. There is a risk that the use of negative advertising can backfire. One form of marketing where people seem willing to take the risk is in politics. It is very common for a politician who is behind in the polls to run negative ads targeting their opponent. Some famous examples include Barry Goldwater's daisy ad, and Hillary Clinton's "3 AM Phone Call" ad from the 2008 primaries.

There are ways to use the Negativity Bias without being overtly negative toward your competitors. For example, you might point out the things your product doesn't do without mentioning your competitor. If you know safety a concern for your customers, you might play up those features in your campaigns. You can imply that your competitors' products don't have the same durability without coming out and saying it.

## The Negativity Bias in Action

Despite the risk associated with using it, the Negativity Bias is still very popular with marketers. Let's start by looking at some examples of the Negativity Bias in B2C marketing:

1. One way to use the Negativity Bias without impugning your competitors is to find a way to make your customers worry, and then reassure them that your product can relieve that worry. Personal hygiene products do this a lot. One classic example is the Scope "Morning Breath" commercial from 1976. The ad featured a sleeping couple. An ominous-sounding voice-over talked about the horror of morning breath. The couple wake up and quickly cover their mouths before hurrying into the bathroom to use Scope. The fear the commercial introduces is that you "have the worst breath of the day" in the morning. Other examples include deodorant commercials and Head and Shoulders shampoo, both of which play on worries about personal hygiene. The benefit of this type of advertising is that it's not merely negative because it offers customers a solution immediately after introducing the worry. .

2. Some companies use the Negativity Bias to attack their competitors with humor. A great recent example of this type of marketing is the Mac vs. PC commercials that

ran a few years ago by Apple. The PC was presented as a middle-aged, stodgy guy while the Mac was hip and young. Apple didn't need to go after a specific company. All they had to do was contrast themselves with a negative image for the ads to be effective.

As you might expect, the Negativity Bias can work for B2B marketing as well:

1. B2B marketers can use the Negativity Bias to draw a contrast between themselves and their competitors. One good example is the State Farm commercials that highlight their quick response time when someone needs to file a claim. The ads featured consumers, not businesses – but State Farm offers business insurance too, and it's a safe bet that those ads boosted their B2B as well.

2. Another effective use of the Negativity Bias for B2B marketing is to talk about negative experiences your customers might have had with other companies. For example, a company that sells business machines might talk about their extended warranty or easy returns, drawing an implicit contrast between themselves and their competitors.

It is important to note that marketers should use care when using negative imagery or wording in their campaigns. Remember, the combination of negative words and imagery may actually have the opposite effect from what was intended. However, if you use it artfully and don't go overboard, the Negativity Bias can be a powerful marketing tool.

## CITATIONS

1. Rosin, P., & Royzman, E. (2001). Negativity Bias, Negativity Dominance, and Cognition. *Personality and Social Psychology Review*, 5, 296-320.
2. Ito, T. A., Larsen, J. T., Smith, N. K., & Cacioppo, J. T. (1998). Negative information weighs more heavily on the brain: the negativity bias in evaluative categorizations. *Journal of personality and social psychology*, 75(4), 887.
3. Liu, B., Jin, Z., Wang, Z., & Hu, Y. (2010). The interaction between pictures and words: evidence from positivity offset and negativity bias. *Experimental brain research*, 201(2), 141-153.

# POST-PURCHASE RATIONALIZATION: WHY DID I BUY THIS?

Have you ever experienced buyer's remorse? If you're like most people, you have. Perhaps you went to a department store that was having a sale. You told yourself you wouldn't spend more than a hundred dollars. While you were there, though, you spotted a pair of boots that you loved. The only problem was that they were priced at two hundred dollars, double the spending cap you'd set for yourself. You tried them on, weighed your options, looked at the original price, and decided they were too good a bargain to pass up.

Later on, when you got home, you looked at your bank balance and though, "I shouldn't have bought those." And very quickly after you said that, you probably started talking yourself into keeping the boots. You told yourself what a great deal they were. You studied the craftsmanship and told yourself you'd have them for the rest of your life, and so on. It might not seem to make sense. It would be more logical to return the boots. The reason you don't is because of a cognitive bias called *Post-Purchase Rationalization*.

## Understanding Post-Purchase Rationalization

Post-Purchase Rationalization has been around for a long time, but it was first formally studied by researchers Joel Cohen and Marvin Goldberg in 1970. In their study, they tested consumers' reactions to coffee they had purchased.[1] One group had exposure to the coffee brand prior to making a purchase, the other did not. The group with the prior exposure had an easier time rationalizing their decision to buy it than the group with no prior exposure.

A 2009 study examined the specific ways that customers rationalize their purchases after the fact.[2] Some of the most common methods included:

- Denial of responsibility (my friends made me do it, it was a one-off, etc.)
- Blame (it's the store's fault)
- Rationalization of long-term usage (I'll get so much use out of it, I can justify the cost over time)

It turns out we're very good at finding excuses to justify what we've done!

Another interesting aspect of Post-Purchase Rationalization was revealed in a study that looked at viewers' reactions to movies.[3] What it found was that the emotions viewers experienced during the movie helped to mitigate any regret they might have had about spending the money to see it.

## Post-Purchase Rationalization in Marketing

Some cognitive biases are used in marketing to convince consumers to buy your product. Post-Purchase Rationalization can be used to overcome indecision on the part of buyers, but it is also effective in minimizing returns and cancelations.

For example, manufacturers of luxury products can use their knowledge of Post-Purchase Rationalization to overcome buyer hesitation. A marketing campaign focusing on quality, uniqueness, and durability can go a long way toward helping customers feel that spending a large amount of money is acceptable.

Another way to ease Post-Purchase Rationalization is to play on consumers' emotions. If you show them images that reflect how they'll feel after they make the purchase, they may be able to call on those images later if they are considering returning the product.

## Post-Purchase Rationalization Examples

Now that you understand what Post-Purchase Rationalization is, let's look at some examples of how to use it in marketing, starting with B2B.

1. Imagine that you sell a high-end B2B product, like software systems or something of that nature. Your clients spend a lot of money to buy your product, and it's not uncommon for them to get a little skittish when they get the bill. You could mitigate that feeling of remorse by sending them an email telling them how smart their purchase was, and outlining the many ways in which it will benefit them. A post-purchase email of this nature helps give your clients exactly what they need to rationalize the purchase.

2. If you find that many clients tend to question their decision after buying your product, you can target your marketing campaign to foster positive emotions.

Remember, the more positive a client's experience is while she's in the sales funnel, the easier it will be for her to rationalize her decision after the fact.

Here are some examples of how to use Post-Purchase Rationalization in B2C marketing:

1.  If you're dealing with customers at the point of purchase, especially when you're selling luxury items, you can make a point of telling them what a great deal they just got. If you've got a mailing list, you can follow up with an email giving them some ways to use the product or featuring some customer testimonials from people who are happy with their purchases.

2.  If you're selling something experiential, like a vacation package or a ticket to an event, put your focus on consumer emotions before, during, and after the event in question. By continually emphasizing positive emotions, you make it more likely customers will enjoy their experience, and less likely that they'll regret it later. Again, this is the type of marketing that could benefit from a follow-up. For example, you might send a survey asking customers about their experience.

3. Finally, you can reduce Post-Purchase Rationalization by providing customers with a coupon or discount code immediately after they make a purchase. Online retailers use this technique all the time. For example, whenever a customer makes a purchase from Café Press, they get a coupon offering them a discount on their next purchase. The coupon acts as a buffer because the customer feels as if they've received something for free, even though they'll have to spend even more to take advantage of it.

Unlike many cognitive biases, Post-Purchase Rationalization is as much about trying to retain customers as it is about attracting new ones. If you use it properly, you can keep your returns to a minimum and increase customer satisfaction with your product.

## CITATIONS

1. Cohen, J. B., & Goldberg, M. E. (1970). The dissonance model in post-decision product evaluation. *Journal of Marketing Research*, 315-321.
2. Chatzidakis, A., Smith, A. P., & Hibbert, S. (2009). .... Do I need it, do I, do I really need this?": Exploring

the role of rationalization in impulse buying episodes. *Advances in Consumer research, 36,* 248-253.

3. Aurîer, P. (1994). The influence of emotions on satisfaction with movie consumption. *Journal of Consumer Satisfaction/Dissatisfaction and Complaining Behavior, 7,* 119.

# RECIPROCITY:
# BUILDING TRUST AND OBLIGATION

I t's the week before Christmas, and you're headed out to a party. You know that some of your friends will be there, and since you routinely exchange gifts with them, you bring their presents with you. You expect that they'll have something for you.

When you get to the party, you see someone who's a friendly acquaintance. In spite of the fact that you've never exchanged gifts before, she has a gift for you. You can feel the blood rush to your face. She knows you brought presents for other people because you've been handing them out all night.

If you're like most people, you're feeling guilty. You feel as if you need to apologize, even though you had no reasonable expectation that she'd have a gift for you. The reason you feel like that is because of a psychological principle called *reciprocity*.

## Understanding Reciprocity

The principle of reciprocity says that people are psychologically more likely to respond to a kind action with a kind reciprocal action. In social terms, that means that when you do a favor for somebody, they are far more likely to be willing to help you out in the future.[1]

In marketing terms, reciprocity is less about favors and more about the exchange of valuable goods. The biggest challenge marketers face is overcoming a buyer's emotional objections to making a purchase. Reciprocity is one way of doing that.

Let's look at one example of reciprocity in marketing that you've probably experienced personally. Imagine that you're shopping at Costco or Trader Joe's. You're a little hungry, and you pass a station where someone is handing out free samples of a product that's on sale. You take a sample. Even if you don't enjoy it, you are far more likely to purchase the product in question than you would be if the store hadn't offered you a preview. The sample fosters a sense of gratitude in you – and in retail, the only way to express gratitude is to make a purchase.[2]

## How Reciprocity Works in Marketing

In terms of marketing, reciprocity can work in several different ways:

1. Offer customers a gift. When you give a potential customer something free, it creates a sense of obligation. You've given him something of value before he's done the same for you. For this type of reciprocity to be effective, it must happen before the customer has pulled out his credit card or laid down cash for a purchase. The chances of a customer making a purchase after accepting a gift are much higher than they would be without the gift.

2. A lot of companies will comp an item or give out coupons when a customer has a negative experience. Unlike the first example, this type of reciprocity happens after an initial purchase, and it's a way of using reciprocity to build trust.[3]

3. Reciprocity can be used with current customers even when they are satisfied. Many brands do things like send out discount codes or special offers using their social media accounts. Instead of customers having

the perception that they're trying to get them to spend money, they see it as the company trying to save them money.[4]

As you can see, reciprocity can be a powerful and versatile tool.

## Reciprocity in Action

Let's look at some real-world examples of reciprocity in action. We'll start with a couple of examples of how B2B companies can use this principle.

- Software companies and subscription services will sometimes offer a free trial membership to new users. It's a great way to get people into your sales funnel, and because you're giving them something for nothing, they're far more likely to stay on with you when the trial period is over.
- Content marketing is another way B2B companies use reciprocity. When a company has a blog that's regularly providing readers with valuable and relevant information, the people who read it will feel the same

sense of obligation they'd feel if they got a free product.

■ Internet marketers often sell to other internet marketers. One of the ways they get visitors to their websites to sign up for their mailing list is to give them a free eBook or other free content. The customer gets the free content, and then the marketer follows up via email to take advantage of the reciprocity effect.

Reciprocity isn't just for B2B marketing. It's just as effective for B2C. Here are some examples:

■ Amazon provides free samples of Kindle books to readers so they can check out an excerpt before they buy. They use a variation of this tactic for print books, too, with their "Look Inside" feature. Both options give customers a sneak peek at the book. It increases their comfort level and makes it easier for them to click the "Buy Now" button when they're done reading the sample.

■ Service-based companies like law firms and accounting firms will often offer new clients a free consultation. They know that hiring a lawyer is a big expense. They know that taking the time to have a 30-minute conversation will do a lot to lower resistance and create a sense of obligation. Clients may be afraid to pull the trigger before the free consult, but they are far more likely to sign on after it happens.

■ BOGO (buy one, get one) offers are another example of B2C reciprocity. A customer who came in to buy a single item sees a sign that if he buys one, he'll get a second one for free. The gratitude he feels for the free item increases the chances that he'll end up buying more than he intended – and he may even buy additional items in the store without realizing why.

If you want to use reciprocity in your marketing efforts, remember that – except in special circumstances where the goal is to build trust with existing customers – the customer should get the free item before making a purchase. When you use it properly, reciprocity can make a big difference in your sales and conversions.

## CITATIONS

1. Regan, D. T. (1971). Effects of a favor and liking on compliance. *Journal of Experimental Social Psychology*, 7(6), 627-639.

2. Palmatier, R., Jarvis, C., & Bechkoff, J. (2009, September 1). The Role of Customer Gratitude in Relationship Marketing. Retrieved July 2, 2015.

3. Raimondo, M. A. (2000, September). The measurement of trust in marketing studies: a review of models and methodologies. In *16th IMP-conference, Bath, UK.*

4. Pervan, S. J., Bove, L. L., & Johnson, L. W. (2009). Reciprocity as a key stabilizing norm of interpersonal marketing relationships: Scale development and validation. *Industrial Marketing Management, 38*(1), 60-70.

# STATUS QUO BIAS:
# LEAVE THINGS THE WAY THEY ARE

Your friend asks you to go out with her while she shops for a new winter coat. As you get dressed to leave the house, you notice that your coat is looking a bit worse for the wear. When you meet her, you say, "I think I'll look for a new coat, too." You wander through the store trying on coats. You find a few that you like, but somehow you can't bring yourself to buy any of them. You're not trying to, but you keep saying things to discourage yourself – things like "It's too expensive" or "White's not a great color for a coat."

At the end of the day, you're not any happier with your old coat than you were, but you've convinced yourself that you can get by using it for one more winter. Your coat isn't any less threadbare than it was earlier in the day, but you've fallen victim to a mental shortcut called the *Status Quo Bias*.

## Understanding the Status Quo Bias

The Status Quo Bias is simple. What it says is that, as a rule, people are inclined to prefer things the way they are over any potential alternative. It was first identified by researchers

Daniel Kahneman, Jack Knetsch and Richard Thaler in their 1991 study about cognitive biases. Their study showed that humans have a predisposition for the status quo, even when the status quo is less than ideal.[1]

The Status Quo Bias is something that affects people in every area of their lives. For example, a 1991 study in the American Economic Review showed that governments were just as susceptive to this bias as people.[2] The Status Quo Bias explains why it is so difficult for governing bodies to make changes, even when it is apparent that the changes would be for the good. The same is true of businesses. If a new employee comes in and makes suggestions to improve efficiency, other employees and management have a tendency to be resistant to change, regardless of the potential improvements that could be brought about it changing.

Another area where the Status Quo Bias affects people is in investments. Consumers have a tendency to stick with their current investment strategy even when there is evidence to suggest that making a change would be advantageous.[3] The bottom line is that the Status Quo Bias tells us that people do not like change.

## The Status Quo Bias in Marketing

The Status Quo Bias is not something to be used in marketing so much as it is something to be overcome. Consumers do not want to change, and if you try to force them to do so, it can backfire in a big way. Perhaps the best-known example of a company that ignored the Status Quo Bias is Coca-Cola. In 1985, Coca-Cola responded to the rising popularity of Pepsi by revamping their classic formula. The reaction was immediate and catastrophic. People hated it. They had no interest in trying a new version of something they already loved. In the end, the new formula of Coke was only produced for one week before the company realized its mistake.

So how can you overcome the Status Quo Bias? There are a couple of things that marketers can do to get customers to make purchases in spite of it. One option is to address the bias head-on. Acknowledge that it's hard to make a change, and then offer the explanation of why now is the time to do it. Another option is to try to get the customer to step into someone else's shoes and look at their choices objectively.

## Examples of the Status Quo Bias

Now that you understand what the Status Quo Bias is and how it works let's take a look at some real-world examples. We'll start with B2C marketing:

1. The Status Quo Bias plays a big role in financial decisions. People tend to be conservative with their money, and they are reluctant to make changes. One example of a finance marketing campaign that worked amazingly well is the Charles Schwab "Talk to Chuck" ads. People might be reluctant to change the status quo, but by making their company seem accessible and approachable, Schwab made it easier for potential clients to make the leap.

2. One way to overcome Status Quo Bias is to introduce the idea of a negative consequence. Online retailer Rue La La uses a counter to show how quickly a particular product is selling out. A customer's reluctance to upset the status quo by making a purchase may be mitigated by her fear of missing out on a great deal.

Overcoming the Status Quo Bias is just as important for B2B marketers as it is for B2C marketers:

1. One aspect of business marketing that can be challenging is convincing potential clients to do something in a new way. For example, when B2B companies started marketing cloud storage options for data, many companies were reluctant to try it. They didn't understand what the cloud was or how it would benefit them. Marketers overcame their bias by offering free trials and discounts so they could try it before making a commitment.

2. Being presented with too many options can sometimes lead decision makers to opt out of making a decision because it seems easier to stick with what they know. One way to work around this is to limit the options available and provide easy-to-read, side-by-side comparisons of products. Best Buy does this for their computers and other electronics, but it could work for almost any product or service.

Dealing with some cognitive biases in marketing is optional. It's not possible to address every possible objection a customer might have at the same time. For many marketers, though, the Status Quo Bias is not one that can be ignored. If you handle it correctly and find ways to alleviate your customers' fear of change, you'll find it easier to make sales.

## CITATIONS

1. Kahneman, D., Knetsch, J. L., & Thaler, R. H. (1991). Anomalies: The endowment effect, loss aversion, and status quo bias. *The journal of economic perspectives*, 193-206.

2. Fernandez, R., & Rodrik, D. (1991). Resistance to reform: Status quo bias in the presence of individual-specific uncertainty. *The American economic review*, 1146-1155.

3. Kempf, A., & Ruenzi, S. (2006). Status quo bias and the number of alternatives: An empirical illustration from the mutual fund industry. *The journal of behavioral finance*, 7(4), 204-213.

# THE AMBIGUITY EFFECT: HOW CAN I BE SURE?

I t's Friday night, and you decide to go to see a movie with friends. You've picked out a movie that appeals to you, and you've checked the reviews. You have a high expectation that you'll enjoy the film you've chosen. But when you get to the theater, your movie is sold out. You now have to choose between two other options that are starting at about the same time. One option is a movie you know got mediocre reviews, and the other is a film you know nothing about it. You decide to see the mediocre movie, even though there's a chance that the other one could be much more enjoyable.

Your decision might seem illogical, but it's actually the result of a cognitive bias known as the *Ambiguity Effect*.

## Understanding the Ambiguity Effect

The Ambiguity Effect was first identified by Daniel Ellsberg in 1961. He conducted an experiment[1] that gave participants two choices. They were presented with an urn containing a total of ninety balls. Thirty of the balls were red while the remaining sixty balls were either black or yellow. They were given a choice between two gambles. In the first, they would win $100 if they picked a red ball out of the urn. In the second, they would get $100 if they chose a black ball. The majority of participants chose Gamble A (the red ball) in spite of the fact that their chances might actually be better if they chose the second option.

The lesson of this experiment, which is also called the Ellsberg Paradox, is that as a rule, people tend to prefer certainty to uncertainty. Participant's in Ellsberg's study knew there was a one-in-three chance that they'd choose a red ball and win the $100, so they selected that option instead of picking one where they were unable to calculate the probability of winning.

## The Ambiguity Effect and Marketing

One of the biggest challenges marketers face is finding a way to clear the cognitive hurdles that prevent consumers from making purchases. The Ambiguity Effect is something that can work against you. If consumers feel that the benefits of choosing your product or service are uncertain, they are more likely to resist making a purchase.

There are a couple of ways marketers can make use of the Ambiguity Effect.

1. When ambiguity exists about your product, you can find ways to minimize it by presenting your advertising in tandem with empirical proof[2] that eliminates some of the uncertainty. For example, let's say you're marketing a weight loss product. Your potential customers likely have some experience with disappointment, and you also know they've got plenty of other options to choose from. You can help eliminate some of the ambiguity in terms of results by presenting statistics or other information. For example, if you say that 90% of people who use your method lose at least ten pounds, you're removing some of the ambiguity and making it easier for people to choose your product.

2. The ambiguity effect works the other way, too. If you don't have statistics or other objective proof to offer regarding your product, you can try to create

ambiguity around your competitor's product instead. An example might be in the area of customer support. Perhaps you're selling software that's similar to your competitor's, but you offer 24-hour chat support and your competitor doesn't. You can highlight the uncertainty of being able to get support when you need it to make it more likely that a customer will buy your software.

3. If you know your customers' tolerance for ambiguity, you can use that information to tailor your marketing campaigns accordingly[3]. If your market research reveals that your customers don't mind some risk – or even enjoy risk – you can use ambiguity to your advantage.

Unlike some cognitive biases, the Ambiguity Effect works both ways. You might not be able to make it work for you, but you can increase the chances that it will work against your competitor.

**Examples of the Ambiguity Effect in Marketing**

Let's take a look at some examples of the Ambiguity Effect in practice in B2C marketing:

1. When marketers don't have facts to back up their claims, they can sometimes use "weasel words" to erase ambiguity. Some examples of this include inexact words and phrases such as: virtually, up to, and as much as. One dishwasher detergent brand claims that dishes will be "virtually spot free." That doesn't mean there won't be any spots – there may or may not be – but by combining a weasel word with a positive claim (spot free) they can influence customers.

2. One way to use ambiguity to your advantage is to use it to highlight negative aspects of your competitor's product. Samsung Galaxy recently used this by running a series of ads referring to iPhone users as "wall-huggers," a reference to the notoriously short life of the iPhone's batteries.

B2B marketers can also make use of the Ambiguity Effect:

1. One of the most effective ways to use the Ambiguity Effect in marketing for business services, especially for established companies, is to highlight experience. If you've got a new competitor in town, you might revamp your ads to say "25 Years Serving Boston"

or something to that effect, thus emphasizing the risk involved with choosing a company with less experience.

2. Insurance companies make good use of the Ambiguity Effect by playing up the risks of not getting insurance. We all know that having proper insurance coverage is important, but increasing coverage and paying a higher premium can seem like an unnecessary expense. If a company highlights the ambiguity of the future by pointing out things that could happen, it can help push businesses to buy additional insurance.

Ambiguity can present challenges to marketers, but if you find ways to work around it, you can make it work to your advantage.

## CITATIONS

1. Ellsberg, D. (1961). Risk, ambiguity, and the Savage axioms. *The quarterly journal of economics*, 643-669.
2. Hoch, S. J., & Ha, Y. W. (1986). Consumer learning: Advertising and the ambiguity of product experience. *Journal of consumer research*, 221-233.

3. Kahn, B. E., & Sarin, R. K. (1988). Modeling ambiguity in decisions under uncertainty. *Journal of Consumer Research*, 265-272.

# THE ANCHORING EFFECT:
## YOU ARE HERE

Imagine yourself in your local supermarket. You've got a list that you made before you left the house, and you've been checking off items as you go. You're nearing the end of your excursion, and you've got just one thing left to buy.

As you near the aisle that holds the canned soup, you glance at your list. It says, "Soup, two cans." When you get to the display, though, you see a sign. It tells you that the soup is on sale for $1.19 per can and that there's a limit of 12 cans per customer.

You came in intending to buy two cans, but if you're like most people, you ended up buying more. A study[1] by psychologists Brian Wansink, Robert Kent, and Stephen Hoch showed that customers who bought soup from a display with no limit bought, on average, 3.3 cans of soup. Customers who bought from the display with the sign advertising the 12-can limit bought an average of 7 cans of soup.

If you recognize this behavior and you're feeling silly, don't. It's incredibly common. The principle at play here is a heuristic known as the *Anchoring Effect*, and you're no more susceptible to it than anyone else.

## Understanding the Anchoring Effect

The anchoring effect, also known as the anchoring heuristic, was first identified in 1974 by cognitive psychologists Amos Tversky and Daniel Kahneman.[2] A heuristic is sort of a mental shortcut – something we rely on to help us simplify complex decisions.

What the anchoring effect says is that, as a rule, we tend to rely heavily on the first piece of information we receive regarding a purchase, even if we don't have any basis to think that it's accurate. The initial information, usually a number, serves as an anchor that we use as a fixed point for negotiations and buying decisions.

One classic example of anchoring happens when you go to a used car lot to buy a car. When you approach a car, the first thing you see is the Manufacturer's Suggested Retail Price

(MSRP.) The price listed is probably too high, but when you see it, it becomes your anchor. As a result, most customers end up looking at any price lower than the MSRP as a good deal, even if they end up paying more than the car is worth.

## How the Anchoring Effect Works

There are a few different ways the anchoring effect can work in marketing. You'll probably recognize all of these as things you've seen in stores or online.

1. Multiple unit pricing. Wansink, Kent and Hoch also studied the ways consumers evaluated prices when products were priced alone or grouped. What they found is that people were more inclined to buy items grouped together than they were stand-alone items. For example, a supermarket might charge one dollar for a roll of toilet paper, or advertise them as "4 rolls for $4." Customers are more likely to buy the bundled items.

2. Quantity limits. This principle is the same as the one we discussed above in the example of the soup cans. When stores set a per customer limit, the number of

items in the limit becomes the anchor for how much the customer will buy.

3. Initial price setting. The MSRP for used cars is an example of initial price setting. Regardless of its reasonableness in terms of the value of the car, the price on the sticker becomes the customer's anchor for negotiations

An interesting thing about the anchor effect is that it holds true even when consumers are specifically warned of its potential to affect them. That's how strong the bias is.

## The Anchoring Effect in Action

Now that you understand the anchoring effect and how it works for everyone – including you – let's take a lot at some examples.

1. One classic way marketers use the anchoring effect is very common in infomercials. You've probably seen several infomercials where, after giving you the run-down on how great their product is, the spokesperson starts asking questions like, "How much would you

pay for this product. Three hundred dollars?" Boom. There's your anchor – three hundred dollars. Regardless of what you thought of the product earlier, you now think that it has a value of three hundred dollars. Then the spokesperson starts to lower the price, and before you know it you're shelling out $49.99 for something you didn't even need because it's such a great bargain. After all, it's worth three hundred dollars. They told you so.

2. You see the anchoring effect on web pages too. A lot of subscription services will have tiered options. A company that's using the anchoring effect will put the highest priced option on the left-hand side of the page, where you'll see it first. Whatever that price is, it becomes your anchor for the remaining prices. The secret here is that they don't expect you to buy that first option. Maybe you will – and if that's the case, great – but its real purpose is to set that anchor for you so that the *next* option seems like a real bargain.

3. One popular way to use anchoring for B2B marketing is by bundling services together.[4] Insurance companies do this by first quoting a price for one coverage (say, property insurance.) The price they quote becomes

the anchor for everything that happens afterwards. A salesperson can then offer to bundle liability insurance with the property coverage, and offer a discount of the client buys both coverages.

4. B2B marketers can also use anchoring by highlighting the fact that the usual price for a product or service is X, but today's price is only Y. The usual price becomes the anchor. When potential clients see it, they feel as if today's price is a bargain. Without the comparison, there would be no way to know whether your usual is a deal or not.

The key to using the anchoring effect is to remember that consumers want something to hold on to. They want a point of reference, and it's your job to give it to them. When you do that, you're in a position of power.

## CITATIONS

1. Wansink, B., & Hoch, S. (1998, February 2). An Anchoring and Adjustment Model of Purchase Quantity Decisions. Retrieved June 29, 2015.

2. Tversky, A., & Kahneman, D. (1974, September 27). Judgment under Uncertain: Heuristics and Biases. Retrieved June 29, 2015.

3. Herrmann, A., Huber, F., & Higie Coulter, R. (1997). Product and service bundling decisions and their effects on purchase intention. *Pricing Strategy and Practice*, 5(3), 99-107.

# THE AVAILABILITY HEURISTIC: SIMPLIFIED DECISION-MAKING

You're getting ready to go on vacation. You've got your tickets, you've started packing, and you're looking forward to getting on a plane and jetting off to a tropical paradise for a week. Two days before you leave, a plane crashes in Japan. It's all over the news. Hundreds of people died, and the media is covering it non-stop. They're showing photographs of smoking wreckage and pictures of the deceased passengers. They're even talking about previous plane crashes.

Suddenly you find yourself dreading the flight. You're not typically a nervous flier, but now all you can think about is that your plane might crash.

The chances of your plane crashing are not any greater than they were before, but the news coverage of the crash has made you susceptible to the *Availability Heuristic*.

## Understanding the Availability Heuristic

A heuristic is a cognitive bias, sort of a mental shortcut that people use to help them evaluate information when it's presented to them. The Availability Heuristic says that when we evaluate a risk or reward, we refer to our memories to find similar experiences. The most readily-available experiences – often the most recent memories – are the ones that have the biggest effect on our decision-making process.

A classic example of the Availability Heuristic comes from a 1973 study[1]. In the study, participants were asked if they thought more words in the English language started with the letter K or had the letter K as the third letter. There are far more words that have the letter K as the third letter, yet the majority of participants said there were more words that began with the letter K. The reason is that it's easier for our brains to recall the first letter of a word than it is to evaluate letter placement within the word.

## The Availability Heuristic in Marketing

One of the most common ways marketers use the Availability Heuristic is to overcome buyer preconceptions and negative experiences. Every customer has personal experiences that may influence her purchasing decisions. For example, a person who's shopping for a financial advisor may have had a very upsetting experience with her previous advisor. She's a little gun-shy, and she's reluctant to trust anyone new. The information about her negative experience is at the forefront of her mind.

A savvy marketer can overcome those objections by introducing a new, positive piece of information to replace the old bias. One very effective way to do that is by telling stories about satisfied customers.[2] When a potential customer hears positive stories about how good the financial advisor's services are, the new stories can replace the old bias, making it more likely that she'll move ahead and sign on as a client.

**Examples of the Availability Heuristic in Action**

Now let's look at some examples of the Availability Heuristic in practice, starting with B2C marketing.

1.  Dating websites tend to show pictures of happy couples on their landing pages and in their advertising. The

pictures trigger the Availability Heuristic by helping consumers to connect ideal outcomes (ecstatic couples embracing) with the product (a dating service.) The probability of finding lasting love through a dating site might be relatively low, but by featuring only the happiest outcomes the site triggers a cognitive bias. People who visit the site are far more likely to sign up for the service when they believe that their chances of a happy outcome are high.

2. State lotteries and casinos use the Availability Heuristic all the time to convince people that their chances of winning are much higher than they actually are.[3] Lottery commercials show smiling winners holding oversized checks and talking about all the things they're going to do with the money they've just won. Casino ads show images of coins cascading from slot machines. The chances of winning are extremely small, but nobody's showing an image of a disappointed person crumpling up a ticket or swearing at a slot machine.

The Availability Heuristic is very effective for B2B marketing as well:

1. Customer testimonials are a very popular way to make use of the Availability Heuristic. A high-end corporate law firm might have video testimonials from satisfied clients talking about how their lawyer helped them avoid paying damages or to settle for a reasonable amount of money. They'll never feature a video of an unhappy client, and the availability of positive testimonials makes it easier for potential clients to sign on.

2. Another way B2B marketers can use the Availability Heuristic is by running ads emphasize one particular aspect of their product or service. Insurance companies make good use of this. For example, State Farm has run a series of commercials touting their 24-hour availability to answer calls and solve problems. The ads play on television, online, and even in movie theaters. They've been very effective in terms of creating a perception that they are more attuned to their customers' needs than other insurance companies.

3. Finally, B2B marketers can use a blog or social media to repeat information about how their product or service solves problems. The repetition makes the information more readily available to potential clients.

When the time comes to make a purchasing decision, the information they are most likely to access is positive, and they're more likely to believe that the company will be able to provide a solution to their problems.

We all have a tendency to think that we have access to a wide range of memories, both good and bad. The truth is that we repeatedly access the same memories. When marketers understand that, they can use the Availability Heuristic to their advantage.

## CITATIONS

1. Tversky, A., & Kahneman, D. (1973). Availability: A heuristic for judging frequency and probability. *Cognitive psychology*, 5(2), 207-232.
2. Folkes, V. S. (1988). The availability heuristic and perceived risk. *Journal of Consumer Research*, 13-23.
3. Schwarz, N., Bless, H., Strack, F., Klumpp, G., Rittenauer-Schatka, H., & Simons, A. (1991). Ease of retrieval as information: Another look at the availability heuristic. *Journal of Personality and Social psychology*, 61(2), 195.

# THE BANDWAGON EFFECT: EVERYONE ELSE IS DOING IT

Have you ever been in a situation where it seemed as if everyone you know had read a particular book? They were all talking about it, but you hadn't read it. In fact, you had no interest in reading it. Maybe you'd even picked it up in a bookstore and read the first few pages, only to put it back on the shelf because you didn't enjoy the writing. After a period during which you felt left out, and friends continued to urge you to read the book, you finally caved in and read it. You didn't enjoy it any more than you thought you would, but you did it anyway.

Why would you read a book you knew you weren't going to enjoy? It's because of a cognitive bias called the *Bandwagon Effect*.

## What is the Bandwagon Effect?

You've probably heard the phrase "jumping on the bandwagon." It's used to describe fans who start following a winning team, or voters who flock to the candidate who's ahead in the polls. In fact, that's where the term originated. Its use dates back to 1848, which a popular circus clown used a bandwagon to attract crowds to his appearances at campaign rallies.

More recently, the term Bandwagon Effect has been used to describe a psychological phenomenon that makes people go with the crowd, even when doing so flies in the face of their personal opinions. A 1994 study[1] examined the effect media coverage has on political campaigns. What it found was that the Bandwagon Effect made undecided voters flock to the perceived frontrunner, regardless of how that person's political beliefs aligned with their own.

Five years later, a second study examined the particular role of the Bandwagon Effect in the purchase of luxury goods.[2] For hedonic purchasing decisions, the determining factor was not the price of the goods, but the prestige that owning them would confer upon the buyer. In other words, when it comes to luxury goods, the Bandwagon Effect is about keeping up with the Joneses.

The Bandwagon Effect is responsible for a lot of fads and trends. Toys are a great example. Think about the huge popularity of things like the hula hoop or Cabbage Patch Dolls. That's the Bandwagon Effect at work.

## The Bandwagon Effect and Marketing

How can marketers take advantage of the Bandwagon Effect? One way is to enable customers to write reviews of products in your online store. Online retailer Amazon has perfected this particular form of marketing.[3] Not only do they encourage customers to leave reviews, they also routinely display messages next to products that say, "Customers who bought this product also bought" with a few suggestions of other items that might go well with the item you're considering.

Another way to use the Bandwagon Effect in marketing is to do whatever you can to make it appear that everyone is buying your product. For example, instead of featuring only a few customer testimonials on your website, you might try putting up dozens. The more you have, the more likely that a potential customer will have that, "Everyone else is doing it, so I will too" attitude.

## Examples of the Bandwagon Effect

The Bandwagon Effect is very popular in marketing. Most people have a tendency toward conformity, even when they prefer to think of themselves as non-conformists. Here are a few examples of the Bandwagon Effect in B2C marketing:

1. Online company Groupon has made very effective use of the Bandwagon Effect. The name of the company even alludes to it – it's a group coupon. Everyone's buying it! Sales of Groupons tend to speed up as the number remaining gets smaller. In other words, people don't want to be left off the bandwagon, so they hurry to buy. It's reasonable to assume that some of those people aren't particularly excited about the offer, they just don't want to be left out.

2. Apple is another company that's used the Bandwagon Effect to its advantage. It's the reason that every time they release a new product, there's a line of people waiting outside their stores to buy it. There's a perception that their products are cool, and that everyone wants to have them. The same, incidentally, has applied to the way people purchase Apple stock.

The Bandwagon Effect can be used in B2B marketing as well. Here are some examples:

1. One of the advantages of using social media for B2B marketing is that it lets you put the Bandwagon Effect to work for you. For example, the more Likes your page has on Facebook, the more probable it is that additional people will Like it. The same goes for Twitter. You can play up this effect by putting social sharing buttons on your blog, which makes it easier for visitors to your site to see how popular your content is.

2. Another way you can use the Bandwagon Effect on your website is to put up a ticker or counter showing how many client you've served, or how much money you've saved them. McDonald's does this in B2C marketing by constantly updating their signs to show the number of customers who have visited their restaurants, but it can work for B2B, too. For example, if you own a law firm, you might put a banner on your website that says, "80% of top local businesses use our services." A statement like that creates the perception that this is the place to be, and that makes it more likely that new clients will choose your firm over the competition.

Most people want to believe that they march to the beat of their own drummer, but the Bandwagon Effect shows how rarely that is the case. When you understand that, you can find ways to promote any business by using it to your advantage.

## CITATIONS

1. Goidel, R. K., & Shields, T. G. (1994). The vanishing marginals, the bandwagon, and the mass media. *The Journal of Politics, 56*(03), 802-810.
2. Vigneron, F., & Johnson, L. W. (1999). A review and a conceptual framework of prestige-seeking consumer behavior. *Academy of Marketing Science Review, 1*(1), 1-15.
3. Sundar, S. S., Oeldorf-Hirsch, A., & Xu, Q. (2008, April). The bandwagon effect of collaborative filtering technology. In *CHI'08 Extended Abstracts on Human Factors in Computing Systems* (pp. 3453-3458). ACM

# THE CONJUNCTION FALLACY: IF THE SHOE FITS

B asic probability is fairly easy to understand – or it should be. The chance of any one particular result is a direct reflection of how many other possible results there are. If you flip a coin, provided that the coin isn't weighted, the probability of heads coming up is 50%, every single time.

The human brain, though, is hardwired to think that specific information affects statistical data. For example, if you're told that someone you're about to meet was a member of Phi Beta Kappa, and then asked what the probability is that he's a mechanic, you would probably guess that the probability is far lower than it actually is because you know about his academic background. It's a common mistake, and it's caused by a cognitive bias called the Conjunction Fallacy.

## Understanding the Conjunction Fallacy

The Conjunction Fallacy was first studied by researchers Amos Tversky and Daniel Kahneman in 1983.[1] In their study, the presented participants with information about a hypothetical person named Linda. They told the participants that Linda was a 31-year-old philosophy major with a deep interest in social justice who had once participated in an anti-nuclear demonstration. They then asked participants to decide which of these two options was more probable:

1. Linda is a bank teller
2. Linda is a bank teller and active in the feminist movement

The basic rules of probability tell us that the chance of Linda being a bank teller is higher than the probability of her being both a bank teller and active in the feminist movement, but the study participants overwhelmingly chose the second option because being active in the feminist movement aligned with the specific information they'd been given about Linda.

A later study showed that introducing priming information (information that helped participants make sense of the options) greatly reduced their susceptibility to the Conjunction Fallacy.[2]

Interestingly, a follow-up study tested participants who were familiar with the Linda study, and even though they knew about the results, they still preferred the experiential option (option 2) over the statistically correct option.

## The Conjunction Fallacy in Marketing

To use the Conjunction Fallacy in marketing, it's important to remember that people put a much higher value on experiential information than they do on numbers. When they were given background information on Linda, it made theme evaluate the information they were given in a different way. Without that information, they would have had no bias in favor of Linda being active in the feminist movement, and thus would have been more likely to choose option 1, which is statistically more probable.

Marketers can use the Conjunction Fallacy by using personal information about a company's founder or employees in marketing. Politicians do this all the time. It's why every presidential convention includes a film about the candidate's life. Voters remember those things more than they do a statistical analysis of her voting record.

Customer testimonials and keeping marketing general can also help.

**Examples of the Conjunction Fallacy**

The Conjunction Fallacy can be a powerful marketing tool, and it can work in multiple ways. Let's look at some examples that might apply to both B2B and B2C marketing:

1. Let's start with politics – campaigning is absolutely a form of B2C marketing! When George W. Bush ran for president, he presented a down-home image that made him seem like a man of the people. He talked about life on the ranch, and, in general, he seemed like the kind of guy people would enjoy spending time with. Statistically speaking, it would be hard to describe someone who grew up in such a wealthy family as a man of the people, but his campaign did a good job of focusing on his personal characteristics so that voters would overlook his relatively elitist upbringing. Politicians of every ideology do this, and it's very effective. You can do the same by putting a personal face on your company and focusing on characteristics that your customers will identify with.

2. Personalize your advertising campaigns. Companies sometimes have a dedicated spokesperson who appears in all of their commercials. When it's done right, that person can become the face of the company. Here's a good example. If you ask most consumers about their opinion of insurance companies, they think of them as impersonal entities, more concerned with making money than anything else. Progressive Insurance has found a way around that by making a character named Flo the centerpiece of their advertising. Flo is warm and approachable, and she makes Progressive seem that way too. The probability of Progressive being any less profit-focused than other insurance companies is small, but Flo makes it seem more likely that they are.

3. Customer testimonials are a great way to use the Conjunction Fallacy. Every company has dissatisfied customers – it's the natural of the business, whatever your business is. Statistically, you might find that 10% of your customers are dissatisfied. You could either present clients with a statistic that says that 90% of your customers are satisfied, or you could forget about the numbers and give them stories from the people who are satisfied. They'll remember the stories more, and even if they end up hearing the statistic

somewhere, they'll give more weight to the personal story than to the numbers.

4. It's also important for marketers not to get caught up in statistical improbabilities themselves. When you're deciding how to segment your market, make sure you're not getting caught up in personal characteristics of your clients. A lot of marketers have a customer persona that they keep in mind when designing campaigns. Don't get so caught up in the specifics of that personal (for example, soccer moms in their 30s) that you forget about other potential markets.

When you use it properly, the Conjunction Fallacy can help your clients to get past negative statistics about your company and give them a way to identify with you on a personal level.

## CITATIONS

1. Tversky, A., & Kahneman, D. (1983). Extensional versus intuitive reasoning: the conjunction fallacy in probability judgment. *Psychological review*, *90*(4), 293.
2. Fiedler, K. (1988). The dependence of the conjunction fallacy on subtle linguistic factors. *Psychological Research*, *50*(2), 123-129.

3. Epstein, S., Donovan, S., & Denes-Raj, V. (1999). The missing link in the paradox of the Linda conjunction problem: Beyond knowing and thinking of the conjunction rule, the intrinsic appeal of heuristic processing. *Personality and Social Psychology Bulletin, 25*(2), 204-214.

# THE DECOY EFFECT:
# MARKETING SLEIGHT OF HAND

Imagine that you're on a website where you're planning to buy a book. Your intention is to buy the eBook version because you figure it'll be less expensive, and you'll be able to start reading it right away on your e-reader. When you click on the title, though, you're presented with three options. One is for the eBook, and the cost is $9.99. The second option is for the print book and the eBook, and the cost is $14.99. The third and final option is for the print book alone, and the cost is $14.99. You started out thinking you would buy the eBook, but you find yourself thinking that getting both versions for only five dollars more is a great deal. You end up choosing that option even though it costs more than the eBook alone – something you would have been happy to get a few minutes ago.

If reading this is making you uncomfortable, don't let it bother you. What happened to you happens to a lot of consumers. It's a psychological principle known as *The Decoy Effect*.[1]

## Understanding the Decoy Effect

The Decoy Effect, also known as the *Asymmetrical Dominance Effect*, says that consumers can be influenced to purchase a higher-priced item when the item in question is clearly superior to a one of the other two choices, even if it is in some way inferior to the third choice.

In general, marketers use the Decoy Effect to drive consumers toward a given option, the one they want them to buy. The example used above is typical. The option to buy only the print version of the book for $14.99 doesn't make sense when viewed side-by-side with the option to get both the print version and the eBook for the same cost. The print-only version of the book is the decoy. The owner of the website wants consumers to choose the print and eBook combination, and is using the Decoy Effect to increase the chances of selling that option.

## How to Use the Decoy Effect in Marketing

There are a couple of different ways marketers can use the Decoy Effect to influence consumer behavior.

1. Include a product or price option that makes a higher-priced option look more attractive. If you had a choice between a car that cost $20,000 and came with a 100,000 mile warranty, and a car that cost $15,000 and came with a 75,000 mile warranty, you might be inclined to choose the second car because it seems like a better bargain. You'll save $5,000 up front. When a third car is introduced, though, the choice becomes trickier. The dealer knows he can make more money selling the first car, so he introduces a third option that costs $23,000 and comes with an 80,000 mile warranty. What happens is that the higher price and lower warranty on the third car cast the first option in a better light. If you choose that option, you can get 20,000 more miles under your warranty for $3,000 less.

2. Retailers can take advantage of the Decoy Effect by shelving products in a clever way. For example, a grocery store might be selling two different versions of their store brand of granola bars. One box has 6 bars for $3.99, and the other one has 12 bars for $7.00. They want you to buy the 12 bars. Next to the box of 12, they might put a different brand that has 10 bars to

a box and costs $7.50. The other brand might include more expensive ingredients or be organic, but in terms of the Decoy Effect, that doesn't matter. What they're hoping customers will do is see the 12-bar box as a better value because it's less than the 8-bar box, even though they're different brands.

## Examples of the Decoy Effect in Action

Let's take a look at some examples of the Decoy Effect in action, starting with B2C marketing:

1. Have you ever been at the concession stand at the movie theater and ordered a small drink? The person working the concession stand points out that the large soda is only fifty cents more than the medium. Even though the large is significantly more than the small soda, it starts to seem like a better deal when compared to the medium size.

2. Some companies that offer travel packages use the Decoy Effect to convince consumers to choose a higher-priced option for their vacation. For example, they might have an option that includes a flight plus

a three-star hotel, and one that offers a flight plus a four-star hotel. With only those two options to choose from, a majority of people would probably go for the lower-priced option with the three-star hotel. If they add a third option for a flight plus a five-star hotel for the same price as the four-star hotel, more consumers will choose the five-star option.[3]

B2B marketers use the Decoy Effect too:

1. Companies that provide business services can steer clients to a higher-priced option by adding a third option that's close to the price of the higher-priced option but has fewer benefits. For example, a financial services company might have a basic service package and a premium package. If they add an intermediary package that is clearly inferior to the premium package, they can steer clients to the premium option because it seems like a better bargain.

2. B2B companies can also use bundling as a Decoy Effect. For example, a software company might offer a download option or a CD-ROM plus download option. They could add a CD-ROM option at only

a few dollars less than the combination option to convince clients to go for the higher-priced choice.

The most common use of the Decoy Effect is in pricing models. When it's done right, it can help you increase sales by changing customers' perception of your prices in relation to one another.

## CITATIONS

1. Zhang, T., & Zhang, D. (2007). Agent-based simulation of consumer purchase decision-making and the decoy effect. *Journal of Business Research*, *60*(8), 912-922.
2. Heath, T. B., & Chatterjee, S. (1995). Asymmetric decoy effects on lower-quality versus higher-quality brands: Meta-analytic and experimental evidence. *Journal of Consumer Research*, 268-284.
3. Josiam, B. M., & Hobson, J. P. (1995). Consumer choice in context: the decoy effect in travel and tourism. *Journal of Travel Research*, *34*(1), 45-50.

# THE FRAMING EFFECT: WHY PRESENTATION MATTERS

It's just after New Year's, and you're shopping around for gym memberships so you can keep your resolution to lose twenty pounds. You find two ads online for local gyms. One tells you that a monthly membership costs twenty-five dollars and the other tells you that you can join for just eighty-three cents a day.

If you're like most people, you went for eighty-three cents a day. You might have even thought to yourself, "That's less than a cup of coffee!"

The catch is that both gym memberships cost the same amount, and you chose the one you did because of a cognitive bias called the *Framing Effect*.

## What is the Framing Effect?

The Framing Effect is a cognitive bias first identified in 1981 by researchers Amos Tversky and Daniel Kahneman.[1]

In their study, they asked presented options for treating a disease that had infected 600 people. In the first frame, they told participants that Option A would save 200 lives while Option B had a 33% chance of saving everybody and a 66% chance of saving nobody. That's the positive frame, and people overwhelmingly chose the first option with its guarantee of saving 200 lives.

In the second frame, they said that Option A would kill 400 people, and that with Option B there was a 33% chance of that all 600 people would live and a 66% chance of that all 600 would die. That's the negative frame. Presenting the information this way made participants choose Option B.

## The Framing Effect in Marketing

In marketing, the Framing Effect is all about which information you choose to highlight. In the example above, the positive frame emphasizes the certainty that Option A will save lives, and the negative frame emphasizes the certainty that it will take lives. The information is identical, but how they presented it changed people's perception of it.

So how can you use the Framing Effect in marketing? Here are some possibilities:

1. A 2007 study[2] showed that customers were more likely to buy private label (generic) products if the emphasis was on the money they would lose by not buying them than on the money they would save by buying them. This is an example of a negative frame.

2. For most consumer products, positive framing is more effective than negative framing. For example, a customer might be more likely to buy ground beef that was advertised as being 75% fat free than she would be to buy the same product if the label said "Contains 25% fat."[3]

3. Sometimes framing an option as a penalty can drive people to take action. For example, instead of offering a lower-priced early registration option for a conference, it might be more effective to present the additional cost for late registration as a penalty.

In simple terms, to use the Framing Effect in your marketing you need to understand which type of frame you customers will respond to.

## Examples of the Framing Effect in Action

The Framing Effect is a cognitive bias that marketers use frequently. It's as common in politics as it is in B2B or B2C marketing. Let's look at some examples:

1.  A 2006 study[4] showed that by framing the way a reward system was presented to customers at a car wash, they could influence the likelihood that customers would collect the reward by making repeated visits to the business. Customers who were given a card that required ten car washes to get a free one with two stickers already in place were far more likely to collect the reward than those who got a card requiring only eight car washes with no stickers on it. Framing the reward system as if the customer had already made progress made the prospect of returning to the car wash more palatable.

2.  Health care companies will often present ads about the need for routine testing by framing them in a negative way. For example, the risk of dying of breast cancer goes up a certain percentage for people who don't get annual mammograms. The way the information

is framed is meant to convince women to schedule an appointment because they fear the consequences if they don't.

3. Framing can be used to negatively influence a customer's opinion about your competitors. For example, a corporate law firm might say in their B2B advertising that they end up settling 80% of their cases out of court. A competitor might point out that 2 out of every 10 of their clients has to endure a costly trial. Using statistics for framing is very popular in politics, as well. It's why presidential candidates tend to throw percentages around in their speeches and debates.

4. One framing tactic that can be very effective for B2B marketing is presenting your product or service in a frame of shared pain or misery. For example, let's say you've developed a new business accounting program. Your advertising might focus on the frustrations you felt with other software that's on the market. Maybe it crashed frequently or lacked certain features. When you talk about your dissatisfaction with other options, you're putting a frame around yourself and your potential client at the same time. The two of you are united in your feelings about other accounting

software. The frame makes it easier for a potential customer to identify with your product – and in turn, more likely to buy it.

5. Another very common framing tactic that can work for any type of marketing is the limited time offer. Internet marketers use this all the time. When someone subscribes to their list, they're redirected to a page that offers them an upsell on a product they just bought that's only available for a short period of time. When an offer is framed as if it's exclusive or might be unavailable soon, a customer is more likely to pull the trigger and buy it.

The Framing Effect can be used in dozens of different ways to highlight features of your product or draw distinctions between you and your competition.

## CITATIONS

1. Tversky, A., & Kahneman, D. (1981). The framing of decisions and the psychology of choice. *Science*, *211*(4481), 453-458.

2. Gamliel, E., & Herstein, R. (2007). The effect of framing on willingness to buy private brands. *Journal of Consumer Marketing, 24*(6), 334-339.

3. Donovan, R. J., & Jalleh, G. (1999). Positively versus negatively framed product attributes: The influence of involvement. *psychology and marketing, 16*(7), 613-630.

4. Nunes, J. C., & Drèze, X. (2006). Your loyalty program is betraying you. *Harvard business review, 84*(4), 124.

# THE HOT HANDS FALLACY:
# ARE WINNING STREAKS REAL?

When there's a big game on, you probably like to get together with your friends and family to watch it. As you watch, you might notice that one player is having a particularly good game. In fact, it seems like every time he gets his hands on the ball, something good happens. He scores or makes a spectacular pass. At some point, you might find yourself saying something like, "Get the ball to Jones. He's got hot hands today."

A statement like that one, "He's got hot hands," is not something that has its roots in logic. If a player has a 60% scoring average, the chances that any one shot will be a scoring shot is 60%. The fact that his last two shots were great doesn't mean that the next one will be – but we believe it, anyway. It's a cognitive bias known as the *Hot Hand Fallacy*.

## Understanding the Hot Hand Fallacy

The Hot Hands Fallacy was first identified by Thomas Gilovich, Amos Tversky and Robert Vallone in 1985.

Their study examined the way people reacted to basketball players. It found that the average person was far more likely to believe that a player would make a shot based on the quality of his previous shots. For example, if a player had shot and scored four times in a row, the study's participants were far more likely to believe that he'd make the next one.[1] This reaction is a cognitive bias because it ignores the laws of probability.

To better understand it, let's look at a related concept: the *Gambler's Fallacy*. The Gambler's Fallacy is the flip-side of the Hot Hand Fallacy. It says that if the same result has occurred many times in a row, the opposite outcome is more likely to occur. The classic example is a coin toss. If heads come up fifty times in a row, the Gambler's Fallacy says you should bet on tails because it's more likely to come up. However, the likelihood of *any one* coin toss resulting in tails is always fifty-fifty, regardless of what happened before.

## The Hot Hand Fallacy and Marketing

Now that you've got a basic grasp of the Hot Hands Fallacy and how it works let's talk about how to use it in marketing.

The most important thing to remember when considering how to use this fallacy in your marketing is that people love a winner. Anything you can do to portray your company or product as being on a winning streak will make consumers more likely to buy it.

Let's start with another research example. A 2005 study tested participants on their stock-purchasing behavior.[2] The study found that consumers were far more likely to purchase a stock that had performed well in the past than one that had performed poorly. The fallacy held even when participants had information that might suggest that the underperforming stock showed the promise of performing significantly better in the future.

Another study – this one slightly disturbing – revealed that consumers would sign up to get advice from a financial advisor who didn't actually exist[3] as long as they thought he had hot hands. That means that the Hot Hand Fallacy is such a powerful cognitive bias that the participants didn't even research the phony financial advisor before making a decision.

## Examples of the Hot Hand Fallacy in Action

The Hot Hand Fallacy can be used in marketing in some surprising ways. Let's start by looking at some B2C examples:

1. A store sells a winning lottery ticket and puts a sign in the window letting the public know about it. Their sales of lottery tickets increase dramatically. Despite the fact that the odds of winning the lottery are infinitesimally small, customers believe that the store in question is more likely to sell them a winning ticket because it happened once before.

2. A personal trainer advertises that he has a 100% success rate in helping people to get in shape. Looking at this situation logically, you can assume that the trainer probably has some skills – but he also most likely attracts highly motivated clients who are willing to put in the work. His success rate makes it more likely that new customers will choose him over another trainer who's not claiming to have hot hands.

B2B marketers can use the Hot Hand Fallacy to their advantage as well:

1. A business consulting firm might take advantage of the Hot Hand Fallacy by repeatedly featuring their biggest success stories in their advertising and on social media. If you were a business owner shopping for a consultant and you saw story after story about how one firm helped its clients to succeed, you'd be far more likely to engage their services than you would a company that didn't seem to be on a winning streak.

2. A law firm that's had a big streak of victories in court could use the streak to advertise their services. In this type of marketing, the specifics are not as important as the streak itself. Potential clients see the streak and believe that their chances of achieving a positive outcome are more likely if they align themselves with someone who's on a hot streak. The law firm's overall success record is far more likely to provide an accurate predictor of the ultimate outcome of the case, but the perception of the streak is enough to convince people to sign on.

As you can see, the key thing to remember when using the Hot Hand Fallacy is that consumers want to believe in streaks. If you can find a way to present your successes as a streak, it will be easier to attract people to your business.

## CITATIONS

1. Gilovich, T., Vallone, R., & Tversky, A. (1985). The hot hand in basketball: On the misperception of random sequences. *Cognitive psychology, 17*(3), 295-314.

2. Johnson, J., Tellis, G. J., & MacInnis, D. J. (2005). Losers, winners, and biased trades. *Journal of Consumer Research, 32*(2), 324-329.

3. Powdthavee, N., & Riyanto, Y. E. (2012). Why do people pay for useless advice? Implications of gambler's and hot-hand fallacies in false-expert setting.

# THE INGROUP BIAS:
# BIRDS OF A FEATHER

Do you remember being in school? If your school was typical, the student body was most likely divided into groups: the cool kids, the jocks, the nerds, the cheerleaders, and the artists, to name a few. Regardless of what group you were in, you and the other people in your group stuck together. A person from another group might be kind and friendly, and you might even have a lot in common with her. But I you're like most people, you probably stuck with your group and viewed everyone else as "other."

Looking back, that behavior might seem silly or unfair, but it's very common, even among adults. We act like that because of a cognitive bias called the *Ingroup Bias*.

## Understanding the Ingroup Bias

Human beings are social animals. Throughout our entire history, we have formed social groups based on criteria that may be superficial or profound. Early humans formed tribes based on blood relations and necessity. Today we group together based on anything from ethnicity to career choices to how we spend our leisure time. The Ingroup Bias was first mentioned in a sociology study conducted by William Sumner in 1906.[1] His research found that human being are hard-wired to form groups, and to favor the members of their own group above members of other groups.

The Ingroup Bias may, in part, be a protective instinct, rather like circling the wagons. We tend to believe that there's safety in numbers and that people who are like us are more likely to have our best interests at heart.

## The Ingroup Bias and Marketing

The Ingroup Bias has several potential applications in marketing and advertising. In general, using people who look like your target customers in advertising and marketing campaigns is a solid strategy. Customers want to identify with the products they buy, and when you present a persona that matches your customer's, you increase the chances they'll buy your product.

A 1999 study[2] studied the way that people who self-identified as ethnic responded to advertising that featured Caucasian actors or ethnic actors. What the researchers found was that ethnic people responded far more positively to ads that featured ethnic people than they did to ads that didn't.

Of course, ethnicity is not the only factor that marketers can use to take advantage of the Ingroup Bias. The tone of your marketing materials can do a lot to help potential customers see your brand as part of their group. For example, if your target audience is women between the ages of 20-40, your brand's voice should reflect that. In other words, talk to potential customers as if you were one of them. Using phrases like "We know what it's like" or "We've been there" can help cement your position as part of their group.

Ingroup Bias can work to build brand loyalty as well. When customers love a brand, they may form groups with other customers who feel the same way.[3] Harley-Davidson is a great example. People who own Harleys get together to talk about their bikes and go on group rides. The group activity reinforces the customers' loyalty to the brand, and also makes the brand itself an honorary member of the group.

## The Ingroup Bias in Action

Marketers use the Ingroup Bias all the time to sell their products and services. Let's look at some examples, starting with B2C marketing:

1. Diet companies and fitness gurus use the Ingroup Bias frequently. Imagine a personal trainer who's lost a ton of weight and now wants overweight people to sign up for his services? He can use the Ingroup Bias by featuring pictures of himself before he lost the weight. His marketing copy might say something like, "I know how frustrated you are because I was there not long ago. Other fitness gurus might make big promises, but I'm the only one who knows what it's really like." Just like that, he's grouped himself with potential clients and increased the chances that they'll sign on with him.

2. Ethnic identification plays a big role in marketing. A tech company who found that not many ethnic people were buying their products might launch a marketing campaign featuring ethnic actors or customer testimonials to appeal to that demographic.

If all of their previous ads featured white actors, it might explain why they've had difficulty selling to other ethnicities.

The Ingroup Bias is equally effective with B2B marketing:

1. One way that companies can use the Ingroup Bias is to do customer research and use what they find to team up with potential clients. For example, if a financial services company learns that most of its clients are environmentally conscious, they might tout the fact that they use paperless reporting and say something like "We share your values" or "Just like you, we're concerned about the planet." Both of those statements, combined with the concrete example of an environmentally friendly service, can help customers feel that you're already on their team.

2. Ethnic identification matters for B2B marketing too. There's a reason so many businesses advertise themselves as "woman-owned" or "minority-owned." Companies who are targeting clients owned by minorities who might speak another language could take advantage of the Ingroup Bias by advertising the

fact that they have someone on staff who speaks the language in question.

3. Using "us vs. them" language can be a very effective way to use the Ingroup Bias, and it can work for almost any industry. The "them" in question doesn't need to be customers who aren't part of your target demographic – it can be your competitors. In other words, "We understand what you need, but they don't." If you combine this kind of language with pictures and testimonials from people or companies in your target demographic, it can pack a powerful one-two punch.

The key to using Ingroup Bias effectively is to understand how your customers or clients identify themselves. Once you know that, you can use that information to frame your product or service in a way that will appeal to them.

## CITATIONS

1. Sumner, W. G. (1906). *Folkways: A study of the sociological importance of usages, manners, customs, mores, and morals*. Ginn.

2. Green, C. L. (1999). Ethnic evaluations of advertising: Interaction effects of strength of ethnic identification, media placement, and degree of racial composition. *Journal of Advertising*, 49-64.

3. Bagozzi, R. P., & Dholakia, U. M. (2006). Antecedents and purchase consequences of customer participation in small group brand communities. *International Journal of Research in Marketing*, *23*(1), 45-61.

# THE MERE EXPOSURE EFFECT: ACQUIRED TASTES

I magine you're in your car. It's the beginning of summer, and you're headed down the highway with the windows on, headed to the beach. You've got the radio cranked up. A new song comes on, and you dislike it as soon as you hear it – so much so that you change the station.

A day or two later, you hear it again. Maybe this time you're at work, and the radio reception is poor, so you don't bother changing the station. You don't like the song any more than you did the first time, but now you've heard the whole thing.

As the summer wears on, the song becomes a smash hit. You can't turn on the radio without hearing it. Not very long after you heard it for the first time, you find yourself headed to the beach again. The song comes on, and you're belting it out at the top of your lungs as you drive.

What happened? It's the same song. You might feel silly if this has happened to you, but you shouldn't. It's the result of a cognitive bias known as the *Mere-Exposure Effect*.

## Understanding the Mere-Exposure Effect

Psychologists have known about the Mere-Exposure Effect for a long time. Researcher Robert Zajonc first identified it in his 1968 study, *Attitudinal Effects of Mere Exposure.*[1] He found that participants' attitudes toward objects became more positive when they received repeated exposure to them. The Mere Exposure Effect is a little like "familiarity breeds contempt" turned on its ear.

He did a follow-up study in 2001 which demonstrated the power of the Mere-Exposure Effect. He found that study subjects did not need to be consciously aware of their exposure to the item in question for the exposure to improve their opinions of it.[2] For example, he experimented with introducing objects on a subliminal level, and found that the effect was the same. It even works pre-natally, which is why doctors tell expectant parents to talk to their babies before they are born.

One important thing to remember about the Mere-Exposure Effect is that the positive benefits of using it are not infinite. There is such a thing as overexposure, as was revealed in a 1990 paper about reputation building.[3] If you expose potential clients to your brand or product too many times, the Mere-Exposure Effect can turn on you and make them less likely to buy. Marketers need to walk a fine line when using this particular cognitive bias.

## The Mere-Exposure Effect in Marketing

Now that you understand the Mere-Exposure Effect let's talk about some ways to use it in advertising. While subliminal images do work, use of them in marketing is frowned upon. However, there are still ways you can use this bias to your advantage.

One of the most obvious ways to use it is by advertising heavily. Frequently when a new product launches, it can feel like you see a commercial for it every two minutes. In the early days of television, companies would sometimes sponsor a show. What that meant was that all of the advertising during the program was from one company. By the end of the broadcast, viewers would be familiar with the product – and having more positive feelings about it than they did before.

Another example of the Mere-Exposure Effect comes from the internet. Although they're not as popular now, banner ads were a very common form of advertising back in the day. The benefit of a banner ad was that it kept your company's name in front of an internet user for a long period – however long they remained on the page where it was displayed. Banner ads may have fallen out of favor, but companies still use things like social media advertising to get the same effect.

**Examples of the Mere-Exposure Effect**

Let's take a look at some examples of the Mere-Exposure Effect in action, starting with B2C marketing:

1. One increasingly popular form of B2C marketing is product placement. That's when a company pays the studio or production company for a film to feature their product in a prominent way. One example that everyone is familiar with is the way the film *E.T.* used Reese's Pieces to lure the little alien out of hiding. Hershey, which makes Reese's Pieces, saw a 65% jump in profits in the two weeks after the movie was released.

2. Another good example of the Mere-Exposure Effect comes from athletic brand Nike. During the 2012 Summer Olympics in London, Nike paid for numerous billboard that appeared around the city with images of young athletes training for the Games. The used the slogan "Find Your Greatness" in conjunction with their distinctive logo. They even integrated social media to ensure they got the highest possible exposure. The connection to the Olympics probably helped prevent a feeling of oversaturation.

The Mere-Exposure Effect can be used in B2B marketing as well:

1. As a rule, potential clients need to see your brand or product seven times before they make a decision to buy. B2B marketers can take advantage of this by using email drip campaigns to keep their name in front of leads. This is a very common tactic with internet marketers in every industry, and it's made easier by the fact that they can use automated systems to send out emails at regular intervals.

2. B2B marketers can harness the Mere-Exposure effect in print advertising too. For example, you might

decide to run an ad several months in a row in a trade publication. The first time it runs it might not get you much business, but after several months it probably will.

3.  Incidentally, B2B marketers can use product placement as well. The Tom Hanks film Castaway was, in many ways, a 2-hour long product placement for FedEx. FedEx markets to other businesses and consumers, and the movie's ending – with Hanks' character delivering a package that he'd kept on the island for years – underlined the company's reliability.

As you can see, the Mere-Exposure is very common in marketing, and for good reason – it works.

## CITATIONS

1.  Zajonc, R. B. (1968). Attitudinal effects of mere exposure. *Journal of personality and social psychology*, *9*(2p2), 1.

2.  Zajonc, R. B. (2001). Mere exposure: A gateway to the subliminal. *Current directions in psychological science*, *10*(6), 224-228.

3. Fombrun, C., & Shanley, M. (1990). What's in a name? Reputation building and corporate strategy. *Academy of management Journal*, *33*(2), 233-258.

# CONCLUSION

Thank you for reading *Unconscious Marketing*. As you can see, cognitive biases help give us a glimpse into the fascinating world that is the human brain. If you think back to the questions we asked about decision making in the introduction, it probably seems a bit funny now that you ever thought that your decision-making process was purely logical. How could it be when your brain knows so many shortcuts and makes so many illogical leaps?

As you read through the explanations and examples in this book, you probably noticed that many of the biases presented have to do with fear.

For example:

- Fear of being left out
- Fear of being in the minority
- Fear of making the wrong choice
- Fear that you already made the wrong choice
- Fear of something improbable

The reason for that is simple. While human thinking and development is, in many ways, light years ahead of where it was in the early days of man, in some ways our brains aren't really very different from the brains of our earliest ancestors. Their primary concern was survival, and the need to survive was at the root of all of their decision making. Is that plant poisonous? Don't eat it. Is that animal going to hurt me? Run from it. Is that storm dangerous? Make a shelter to hide from it. They're all very simple decisions driven by the same simple goal: to stay alive.

For most people, running from wild animals or accidentally eating a poisonous plant aren't real concerns today. Instead of gathering food in the forests or fields, we find it – neatly picked and washed – in refrigerated cases in our local supermarket. We may occasionally find ourselves in the presence of a wild animal, but it's usually at a zoo and there's almost no chance we'll get hurt.

The fact that our lives are so much safer now, though, hasn't gotten through to our brains. We still have a pretty significant amount of real estate in our brains that's given over to survival. In the absence of daily life-or-death situations, we still live in fear a lot of them time – even if we're not consciously aware of it. When we waver over a purchasing decision, we're thinking about whether or not we should spend the money, or wondering if they product we're considering will work the way we think it will. Even though the fear or worry we feel is not a matter of survival, our brains still feel like it is. They still react as if it is – and that's why cognitive biases are so hard to shake.

When you're considering which cognitive bias or biases to use in a particular marketing campaign, start by thinking about your target customer. Who is she? What are her biggest fears? What can you do to assuage those fears? Remember, most people don't go into a purchasing decision feeling afraid in a conscious way. It's far more subtle than that. Their fears exist mostly on a subconscious level, and most people would probably deny that they felt fear if you asked them directly.

Once you understand what a customer's fears are, you can work backward and figure out which cognitive bias is most likely to get you the result you want. For example, if you know that your target customer fears being thought of as incompetent, you might use the IKEA Effect and incorporate a "do-it-yourself" aspect into your product or service. On the other hand, a customer who's very confident might not be susceptible to that, but he might be susceptible to a fear of things changing. In that case, a campaign making use of the Status Quo Bias might be your best bet.

As you can see, understanding your customers is crucial. If you lack a basic understanding of who is buying your product and why they're buying it, you won't be able to craft an effective marketing campaign. Customer research is the key. If you're clever about it, you can use things like social media and customer surveys to get customers to tell you exactly which biases they are most susceptible to. The key is asking the right questions, and knowing how to interpret the answers.

The examples and suggestions in this book are only a small taste of what you can do once you start using cognitive biases in your marketing. As you move forward, pay attention to every commercial or marketing campaign you see. Notice how other marketers are making use of cognitive biases, and take notes. It may be especially effective to look at your competitors' campaigns and see if they are missing opportunities to employ cognitive biases in their marketing. Part of marketing is finding ways to win customers away from the competition, and with the tools you have now, you may be able to find weaknesses in others' advertising that you can use to your advantage.

You may find that some of the cognitive biases discussed in this book don't apply to you, while others may end up being like reliable friends that you can make use of in countless campaigns as you move forward. Each bias can be used in a multitude of ways, and the only real limits are the limits of your imagination.

One thing that may be particularly helpful as you become accustomed to using cognitive biases in your marketing is to test different ways of using them. These are new tools for you, so don't be afraid to experiment and try different things. The more comfortable you get using them, the more effective your campaigns will be.

# ABOUT THE AUTHOR

Sam Page is the CEO and founder of NeuroTriggers Agency, the world's only full service neuromarketing firm. With a Master's degree in Psychology, coupled with an MBA, Sam recognizes better than most that effective business development hinges on the science of human behavior. His company develops campaigns which directly tap into to the thoughts, feelings, and beliefs of his clients' target market. This is reflected in his three step Profit Engineering formula:

**Understand - Connect - Grow**

Sam's philosophy is that marketing's greatest battles aren't won or lost in your store, in the street, or on the web... they're won or lost inside the mind of your customer. With 10 years "in the trenches" experience in direct sales and marketing, he's been responsible for generating millions in revenue for some of the world's most successful owner-operated businesses. Born and raised in Australia, he takes a no-holds barred approach to re-engineering business development systems.

# FREE RESOURCES FROM SAM PAGE AND THE NEUROTRIGGERS TEAM

As an expression of gratitude for reading this book, I would like to offer you two FREE gifts so you can leverage the power of marketing psychology in your own business.

- **Visual Impact Map.** How well does your website engage your users' reptilian brain? Using predictive analysis, we'll present a full color map outlining your website's primary engagement points. *(Normally $129)*.
- **Follow-up consultation and discovery session** (with a licensed consumer psychologist) to review your neuromarketing score. *(Normally $250)*.

To claim these FREE gifts, just head on over to our website at www.NeuroTriggersAgency.com or shoot us an email at support@NeuroTriggersAgency.com.

CPSIA information can be obtained
at www.ICGtesting.com
Printed in the USA
LVOW01s2200230716

497536LV00031B/844/P